Praise for *Advice Not Given*

"Most people will never find a great psychiatrist or a great Buddhist teacher, but Mark Epstein is both, and the wisdom he imparts in *Advice Not Given* is an act of generosity and compassion. The book is a tonic for the ailments of our time."

—Ann Patchett, *New York Times* bestselling
author of *Commonwealth*

"Mark Epstein's *Advice Not Given* continues his important, fascinating work in exceptionally lucid language. It also offers its readers a collection of fables, vignettes, and personal revelations with the true capacity to rearrange one's perspective, even change one's life. I suspect many of these offerings will stay with me for the long haul, for which I'm very grateful."

—Maggie Nelson, *New York Times* bestselling
author of *The Argonauts*

"Epstein's book of practical suggestions will leave readers educated, inspired, and equipped with new tools for psychological health."

—*Publishers Weekly* (starred review)

"Epstein writes with lightness and reverence. There's a sense of equanimity and deep trust in the experience of life that's palpable. If you've always wanted to develop a relationship with a kind and reassuring psychiatrist, one who knows your every thought and still accepts you, *Advice Not Given* will give you a taste of that sort of relationship. You'll feel a sense of ease and an acceptance of yourself, and for what did and didn't happen—and for what was and wasn't said." —PsychologyToday.com, "The Clarity"

"In *Advice Not Given* Mark Epstein shares his remarkably practical wisdom, borne of a brilliant interchange between the fundamentals of Buddhism and the insights of psychotherapy. We all can benefit from this advice, given here freely."

—Daniel Goleman, *New York Times* bestselling author
of *Altered Traits* and *Emotional Intelligence*

"There are psychologists influenced by Buddhism and Buddhists influenced by psychology, and then there is Mark Epstein, whose deep and humane reflections on healing and self-understanding weave these two great disciplines into a lovely and nuanced whole. As in his other books, only this time more personally and more passionately, Epstein in *Advice Not Given* offers the reader a rare intelligence and honesty. A pleasure to read and contemplate!"
—Norman Fischer, poet, Zen priest, and author of *What is Zen?*

"An integrative pioneer who has done more than anyone to bridge Buddhism with Western psychotherapy, Mark Epstein has now given us a fine distillation of his work, exemplified by revealing insights from his life and practice. Written in spare and elegant prose, *Advice Not Given* urges us toward the discoveries and unexpected sources of consolation that each tradition offers. A memorable experience." —George Makari, author of *Soul Machine*

"*Advice Not Given* is a beautiful reminder of what matters; intimate, moving, insightful, tender, and tough. It invites me to a wiser mind and an open heart." —Jack Kornfield, author of *A Path with Heart*

"In times of strife, with a nation divided, and the dire consequences of a warming world sweeping over our lives, Mark Epstein is always there to provide us with a roadmap for a journey of transformation, a pilgrim's path where the goal is not a place but a state of mind, not a destination but an all embracing state of peace, salvation and liberation. He is America's physician of the psyche, healer of the mind, avatar of the heart."
—Wade Davis, author of *The Serpent and the Rainbow*

"Mark Epstein's *Advice Not Given* is a truly wonderful book—it held me in its intelligent, kind, and lucid grip all the way through, and gave me back to the world at the end a refreshing bit more over myself. I can see Buddha and Freud smiling to each other, pleased about what a gracious insight their partnership in mentoring Dr. Mark had enabled him to bring about and offer to us all in such a

work. I cannot recommend this work highly enough to anyone who wants to take better notice of what makes human life so exquisitely worthwhile. A true treasure of a guide to being real."
      —Robert A. F. Thurman, Jey Tsong Khapa Professor of Buddhism
         at Columbia University and author of *Man of Peace*

"Extraordinary. Mark Epstein does a remarkable job in bringing together the traditions of Buddhism and psychotherapy into an immensely useful book for our time."
      —Roshi Joan Halifax, Abbot of Upaya Institute and
         Zen Center and author of *Being with Dying*

"Mark Epstein interweaves psychotherapy and Buddhism in ways that help readers further their own personal growth and practice. At once down to earth, caring, suggestive, a sharing of years of work in the front lines of his own person and helping others."
      —Michael Eigen, author of *Feeling Matters*, *Faith*,
         and *The Psychoanalytic Mystic*

"For those looking to explore the idea of a Buddhist psychology in greater depth, Epstein has been writing on the topic since his first book was published in 1995. *Advice Not Given* is one of his best to date and a perfect place to start."   —PsychologyToday.com

PENGUIN BOOKS

ADVICE NOT GIVEN

Mark Epstein, M.D., is a psychiatrist in private practice in New York City and the author of a number of books about the interface of Buddhism and psychotherapy, including *The Trauma of Everyday Life*, *Thoughts without a Thinker*, and *Going to Pieces without Falling Apart*. He received his undergraduate and medical degrees from Harvard University.

Advice Not Given

A Guide to Getting Over Yourself

MARK EPSTEIN, M.D.

PENGUIN BOOKS

PENGUIN BOOKS

An imprint of Penguin Random House LLC
375 Hudson Street
New York, New York 10014
penguinrandomhouse.com

First published in the United States of America by Penguin Press,
an imprint of Penguin Random House LLC, 2018
Published in Penguin Books 2018

A portion of Chapter 3 first appeared under the title "The Trauma of Being Alive" in
The New York Times, August 3, 2013, and a portion of Chapter 6 appeared as
"Beyond Blame" in *Tricycle: The Buddhist Review*, Summer 2009.

Excerpt from "The Sword in the Stone" from *Faithful and Virtuous Night* by Louise Glück.
Copyright © 2014 by Louise Glück. Reprinted by permission of Farrar, Straus and Giroux
and Carcanet Press Limited.

ISBN 9780399564345 (paperback)

THE LIBRARY OF CONGRESS HAS CATALOGED THE HARDCOVER EDITION AS FOLLOWS:
Names: Epstein, Mark, 1953– author.
Title: Advice not given : a guide to getting over yourself / Mark Epstein, MD.
Description: New York : Penguin Press, [2018] |
Includes bibliographical references and index.
Identifiers: LCCN 2017025261 (print) | LCCN 2017037517 (ebook) |
ISBN 9780399564338 (ebook) | ISBN 9780399564321 (hardcover)
Subjects: LCSH: Buddhism—Psychology. | Psychotherapy—Religious
aspects—Buddhism. | Egoism—Religious aspects—Buddhism. | Buddhism—Doctrines.
Classification: LCC BQ4570.P76 (ebook) | LCC BQ4570.P76 E662 2018 (print) |
DDC 294.3/444—dc23
LC record available at https://lccn.loc.gov/2017025261

Printed in the United States of America
1 3 5 7 9 10 8 6 4 2

Designed by Amanda Dewey

For Arlene

Praise and blame, gain and loss, pleasure and sorrow come and go like the wind. To be happy, rest like a giant tree in the midst of them all.

THE BUDDHA

Author's Note

Except in the case of those introduced by first and last names, I have changed names and other identifying details or constructed composites in order to protect privacy.

A paragraph of Chapter 1 and a portion of Chapter 3 first appeared in the *New York Times* on August 3, 2013, under the title "The Trauma of Being Alive." A portion of Chapter 6 first appeared in the summer 2009 issue of *Tricycle: The Buddhist Review* under the title "Beyond Blame."

CONTENTS

Advice Not Given

INTRODUCTION

Ego is the one affliction we all have in common. Because of our understandable efforts to be bigger, better, smarter, stronger, richer, or more attractive, we are shadowed by a nagging sense of weariness and self-doubt. Our very efforts at self-improvement orient us in an unsustainable direction since we can never be certain whether we have achieved enough. We want our lives to be better but we are hamstrung in our approach. Disappointment is the inevitable consequence of endless ambition, and bitterness a common refrain when things do not work out. Dreams are a good window into this. They hurl us into situations in which we feel stuck, exposed, embarrassed, or humiliated, feelings we do our best to keep at bay during our waking hours. Our disturbing dreams are trying to tell us something, however. The ego is not an innocent bystander. While it claims to have our own best interests at heart, in its relentless pursuit of attention and power it undermines the very goals it sets out to achieve. The ego needs our help. If we want a more satisfying existence, we have to teach it to loosen its grip.

There are many things in life we can do nothing about—the circumstances of our childhoods; natural events in the outer world; the chaos and catastrophe of illness, accident, loss, and abuse—but there is one thing we *can* change. How we interact with our own egos is up to us. We get very little help with this in life. No one really teaches us how to be with ourselves in a constructive way. There is a lot of encouragement in our culture for developing a stronger sense of self. Self-love, self-esteem, self-confidence, and the ability to aggressively get one's needs met are all goals that most people subscribe to. As important as these accomplishments may be, however, they are not enough to guarantee well-being. People with a strong sense of self still suffer. They may look like they have it all together, but they cannot relax without drinking or taking drugs. They cannot unwind, give affection, improvise, create, or sympathize with others if they are steadfastly focused only on themselves. Simply building up the ego leaves a person stranded. The most important events in our lives, from falling in love to giving birth to facing death, all require the ego to let go.

This is not something the ego knows how to do. If it had a mind of its own, it would not see this as its mission. But there is no reason for the untutored ego to hold sway over our lives, no reason for a permanently selfish agenda to be our bottom line. The very ego whose fears and attachments drive us is also capable of a profound and far-reaching development. We have the capacity, as conscious and self-reflecting individuals, to talk back to the ego. Instead of focusing solely on success in the external world, we can direct ourselves to the internal one. There is much self-esteem to be gained from learning how and when to surrender.

While our culture does not generally support the conscious de-escalation of the ego, there are silent advocates for it in our midst. Buddhist psychology and Western psychotherapy both hold out hope for a more flexible ego, one that does not pit the individual against everyone else in a futile attempt to gain total surety. These two traditions developed in completely different times and places and, until relatively recently, had nothing to do with each other. But the originators of each tradition—Siddhartha Gautama, the South Asian prince who renounced his luxurious lifestyle to seek an escape from the indignities of old age, illness, and death; and Sigmund Freud, the Viennese doctor whose interpretation of his own dreams set him on a path to illuminate the dark undercurrents of the human psyche—both identified the untrammeled ego as the limiting factor in our well-being. As different as these two individuals were, they came to a virtually identical conclusion. When we let the ego have free rein, we suffer. But when it learns to let go, we are free.

Neither Buddhism nor psychotherapy seeks to eradicate the ego. To do so would render us either helpless or psychotic. We need our egos to navigate the world, to regulate our instincts, to exercise our executive function, and to mediate the conflicting demands of self and other. The therapeutic practices of both Buddhism and psychotherapy are often used to build up the ego in just these ways. When someone is depressed or suffers from low self-esteem because he or she has been mistreated, for example, therapy must focus on repairing a battered ego. Similarly, many people have embraced the meditation practices of the East to help build up their self-confidence. Focus and concentration diminish stress and anxiety and help people adapt to challenging home and work environments. Meditation has found a place in hospitals, on Wall Street, in the armed forces, and in sports arenas, and much of its benefit lies in the ego strength it confers by giving people more control over their minds and bodies. The ego-enhancing aspects of both of these approaches are not to be minimized. But ego enhancement, by itself, can get us only so far.

Both Western psychotherapy and Buddhism seek to empower the observing "I" over the unbridled "me." They aim to rebalance the ego, diminishing self-centeredness by encouraging self-reflection. They do this in different, although related, ways and with different, although related, visions. For Freud, free association and the analysis of dreams were the primary methods. By having his patients lie supine and stare into space while saying whatever came to mind, he shifted the usual equilibrium of the ego toward the subjective. Although few people lie on the couch anymore, this kind of self-reflection remains one of the most therapeutic aspects of psychotherapy. People learn to make room for themselves, to be with uncomfortable emotional experiences, in a more accepting way. They learn to make sense of their internal conflicts and unconscious motivations, to relax against the strain of the ego's perfectionism.

Buddhism counsels something similar. Although its central premise is that suffering is an inextricable aspect of life, it is actually a cheerful religion. Its meditations are designed to teach people to watch their own minds without necessarily believing everything they think. Mindfulness, the ability to be with whatever is happening in a moment-to-moment way, helps one not be victimized by one's most selfish impulses. Meditators are trained to not push away the unpleasant nor cling to the pleasant but to make room for whatever arises. Impulsive reactions, in the form of likes and dislikes, are given the same kind of attention as everything else, so that people learn to dwell more consistently in their observing awareness, just as one does in classic modes of therapy. This observing awareness is an impersonal part of the ego, unconditioned by one's usual needs and expectations. Mindfulness pulls one away from the immature ego's insistent self-concern, and in the process it enhances one's equilibrium in the face of incessant change. This turns out to be enormously helpful in dealing with the many indignities life throws at us.

While the two approaches are very similar, the primary areas of concern turned out to be different. Freud became interested in the roiling instincts and passions that rise to the surface when the ego is put under observation. He saw himself as a conjuror of the unconscious, an illuminator of the dark undercurrents of human behavior. When not prompted, people reveal themselves, often to their own surprise, and what they discover, while not always pretty, gives them a deeper and richer appreciation of themselves. Out of the dark earth, after a night's rain, flowers grow. Freud took delight in poking fun at the belief that we are masters in our own houses, comparing his discoveries to those of Copernicus, who insisted that the sun does not revolve around the earth, and Darwin, who claimed that man "bears in his bodily frame the indelible stamp of his lowly origin." For Freud, the ego could evolve only by giving up its ambitions of mastery. The ego he encouraged was a humbled one, wider in scope but aware of its own limitations, not driven so much by instinctual cravings but able to use its energies creatively and for the benefit of others.

While maintaining a similar reliance on self-observation, Buddhism has a different focus. It seeks to give people a taste of pure awareness. Its meditation practices, like those of therapy, are built on the split between subject and object. But rather than finding uncovered instincts to be the most illuminating, Buddhism finds inspiration in the phenomenon of consciousness itself. Mindfulness holds up a mirror to all the activity of mind and body. This image of the mirror is central to Buddhist thought. A mirror reflects things without distortion. Our consciousness is like that mirror. It reflects things just as they are. In most people's lives, this is taken for granted; no special attention is given to this mysterious occurrence. But mindfulness takes this knowing consciousness as its most compelling object. The bell is ringing. I hear it and on top of that I know that "I" am hearing it and, when mindful, I might even know that I know that I am hearing it. But once in a while in deep meditation, this whole thing collapses and all that is left is one's mirrorlike knowing. No "I," no "me," just pure subjective awareness. The bell, the sound, that's it! It is very hard to talk about, but when it happens the freedom from one's usual identity comes as a relief. The contrast with one's habitual ego-driven state is overwhelming, and much of the Buddhist tradition is designed to help consolidate the perspective of this "Great Perfect Mirror Wisdom" with one's day-to-day personality.

But this perspective is notoriously difficult to integrate, the consolidation with the personality hard to achieve. Even the Buddha was said to have trouble. The legendary story of his life is illuminating in this regard. Born a prince, he grew up in a family that did everything it could to protect him from confronting old age, illness, and death. He married and had a son, but caught his first glimpses of an old person, a sick person, and a corpse at the age of twenty-nine while riding in the countryside beyond the palace walls. These images so unnerved him that he left his loving family to go on a spiritual quest in the wilds of the Indian subcontinent. After years of self-examination, meditation, and ascetic practices, he broke through his selfish preoccupations and saw how he was contributing to his own suffering. Awakening followed quickly thereafter.

Before his enlightenment, the Buddha did battle with a fearsome and wily god named Mara, who represented his ego. Mara tried to sway him from his path by appealing to his latent desires for sex and power. He flattered the Buddha and promised him that he could be a great ruler if he but abandoned his quest, sending his daughters to seduce him and his armies to engage and distract him. The Buddha never relented and achieved his breakthrough despite Mara's valiant attempts to dissuade him. But even after the Buddha's enlightenment, Mara remained a force to reckon with. He continued to whisper to the Buddha about all the fame and fortune he deserved, about the pointlessness of his personal sacrifice. The Buddha had to deal with his own ego even after his enlightenment. This is an aspect of Buddhist thought that dovetails nicely with psychotherapy. Relaxing the ego's grip makes the experience of pure awareness possible, but the experience of pure awareness makes it clear what work still needs to be done on the ego. After the ecstasy, it is said, comes the laundry.

This is described very clearly in a famous Buddhist fable. An aged Chinese monk, despairing at never having reached enlightenment, asks permission to go to an isolated cave to make one final attempt at realization. Taking his robes, his begging bowl, and a few possessions, he heads out on foot into the mountains. On his way he meets an old man walking down; the man is carrying a huge bundle. Something about him suggests wisdom to the troubled monk. "Say, old man," the monk says, "do you know anything of this enlightenment I seek?" The old man drops his bundle to the ground. Seeing this, the monk is instantly enlightened. "You mean it is that simple?" he asks. "Just let go and not grasp anything!" But then he has a moment of doubt. "So now what?" he asks. And the old man, smiling silently, picks up his bundle and walks off down the path toward town.

The message is clear. Awakening does not make the ego disappear; it changes one's relationship to it. The balance of power shifts, but there is still work to do. Rather than being driven by selfish concerns, one finds it necessary to take personal responsibility for them. In Buddhism, this engagement with the ego is described as both the path *to* enlightenment and the path *out of* it. It is traditionally explained as an Eightfold Path: Right View, Right Motivation, Right Speech, Right Action, Right Livelihood, Right Effort, Right Mindfulness, and Right Concentration. To counter the persistent and insidious influence the ego has on us—called "self-grasping" in Buddhist thought—one has to be willing to work with it on all eight levels: before awakening *and* after.

The Eightfold Path was one of the Buddha's original organizing principles. He spoke of it in the first teaching he ever gave and referred to it often thereafter. Buddhism has morphed and developed in the twenty-six hundred years since the Buddha taught in ancient India. It spread through India, moved to China, Southeast Asia, Indonesia, Tibet, Korea, and Japan, changing form and evolving many different schools of thought as it made its way through time and space. But the Eightfold Path has remained a constant. While Right Effort, Concentration, and Mindfulness refer primarily to meditation, the other branches do not. Right View and Right Motivation speak to the role of insight in countering the ego's insistent demands, while Right Speech, Action, and Livelihood describe the importance of ethical restraint in thwarting the ego's selfish impulses.

The eight branches of the Eightfold Path make up the chapters of this book. While they are as old as Buddhism itself, when informed by the sensibility of Western psychotherapy they become something more. A road map for spiritual and psychological growth, they are also a way of dealing with the intractable and corrosive problem of the ego. While no single therapeutic approach has a monopoly on truth, in a world increasingly dominated by the Western regard for individual ambition, the dangers of an unbridled ego need to be acknowledged. This is not the approach our culture generally takes, but it is something we can all use. To move our psychologies to a better place, we must look at the hold our egos have over us.

This kind of advice does not apply only in the West. While psychotherapy has never been a strong tradition in the East, this does not mean that people in Eastern cultures are not subject to all of the same conflicts and defenses as Westerners. There are certainly many people in Buddhist cultures who have used meditation to evade themselves, who have never really confronted the tenacity of the ego's grip. I was told recently about one such person, a hermit who, after meditating in a cave in the mountains of Nepal, heard that the Dalai Lama would soon be passing through his remote area. The Dalai Lama, in the tradition of Tibetan Buddhism, is the most highly regarded spiritual figure in the culture. He is considered a pure expression of enlightened wisdom, and any chance to be in his compassionate presence, let alone to meet with him, is virtually irresistible to those who revere him. This hermit had mastered many of the classic meditations designed to quiet the mind and calm anxiety. Villagers brought him food to keep him healthy, but other than these rare encounters he had been alone for four years in deep states of meditation. He somehow arranged for a personal meeting with the Dalai Lama and emerged from his self-imposed retreat for the encounter. He asked the Dalai Lama for advice on what to do next.

The Dalai Lama, who fled his native Tibet in 1959 when the Chinese invaded, has spent much of his adult life in dialogue with the West. I visited his place of exile in the foothills of the Indian Himalayas in 1977 before I started medical school and returned for six weeks on a research grant before I graduated in 1981. I have had the opportunity to hear him teach on many occasions since. When he speaks about meditation, he often makes a distinction between practices that quiet the mind and those that utilize the mind's intelligence for its development. Many people, in both the East and the West, believe that shutting down the ego, and the thinking mind, is the ultimate purpose of meditation. The Dalai Lama, rather forcefully, always argues that this is a grave misunderstanding. Ego is at once our biggest obstacle and our greatest hope. We can be at its mercy or we can learn to mold it according to certain guiding principles. Intelligence is a key ally in this shaping process, something to be harnessed in the service of one's progress. The Dalai Lama's advice to the hermit seemed to spring from this place.

"Get a life," the Dalai Lama admonished him.

This monk, from a poor Nepalese village, was shaken by the exchange. It went against all his preconceived notions of what a monk should do. The Dalai Lama was not negating the value of the hermit's meditations, but, like the old man in the Buddhist fable, he did not want his student to stop there. It was time to pick up his bundle and return to town rather than resting on the laurels of his spiritual attainments.

The hermit had a sister who had been taken in the sex trade. The Dalai Lama's advice motivated him to emerge from his cave and begin providing education and health care for local village women. An acquaintance of mine helped to fund some of this work, and he was present when someone reminded the Dalai Lama of this pivotal exchange.

The Dalai Lama chuckled. "Oh, yes," he said proudly. "I told him, 'Get a life.'"

The Dalai Lama's advice, while cryptic enough to fit with his role as a Buddhist master, comes from a place of age-old wisdom, as relevant in the West as it is in the East, as helpful today as it was in the time of the Buddha, as true for us as it was for the Nepalese monk.

We all have a life, but we are not always aware of how precious it is. And we all have an ego, but we do not always take enough responsibility for it. Our sufferings, or our doomed attempts to avoid them, all too often keep us mired in obsessive attachment, greed, worry, or despair. There are those, like the hermit in Nepal, who are attracted to spiritual pursuits because they seek a means of escape from life. They view enlightenment as a way out. But this attempt to leapfrog over the ego is counterproductive. There is no getting around it. If we wish to not perpetuate suffering, we have to take a hard look at ourselves. Making one's life into a meditation is different from using meditation to escape from life.

This book is a how-to guide that refuses a quick fix. It is rooted in two traditions devoted to maximizing the human potential for living a better life—traditions that have only begun to speak to each other. Although the conversation is just starting, it is clear that Buddhism and Western psychotherapy have much in common. They each recognize that the key to overcoming suffering is the conscious acknowledgment of the ego's nefarious ways. Without such consciousness, we remain pushed around by impulses and held in check by unrecognized defenses. But when we are able to see the extent of our own fears and desires, there is something in us, recognized by both Buddha and Freud, which is able to break free. Taking responsibility for what is going on inside of us gives hope.

One Caveat

I had the unusual—and I would say fortunate—experience of discovering Buddhism before I knew very much about anything else, certainly before studying Western psychology or deciding to go to medical school to be trained as a psychiatrist. Buddhism spoke to me personally from the start. The very first verse of the Buddha I ever read (in a college survey class in my freshman year) was about training the anxious mind. I felt an immediate attraction to it, as if the words were written just for me. Soon I found myself in the bowels of the university library digging out ancient Buddhist texts buried deep in the library's stacks. Many of these books had not been checked out for years, but this made them seem all the more special to my eyes.

There was a map of the mind in those ancient texts that seemed relevant to me. This map charts a path whereby the mind can be developed, where qualities like kindness, generosity, humor, and empathy can grow out of a willingness to question one's own instinctive attractions and aversions. The inner peace of a calm mind, the satisfaction of creative expression, the solace and joy of enduring relationships, the gratification of helping and teaching others, and the liberation of seeing past one's own selfish concerns into other people's welfare began to seem like realistic goals, goals that an engagement with Buddhism might make more achievable. I wrote an undergraduate thesis on this ancient Buddhist map that continues to inform my work to this day. I met my first meditation teachers before my twenty-first birthday and "sat" my first two-week silent retreat shortly thereafter. Although I struggled with meditation—for something so simple, it is remarkably difficult—it came alive for me in that first two-week course, and I have returned to these retreats dozens of times since. Every retreat has shown me something interesting about myself and reinforced my initial enthusiasm. Meditation is a real thing. If you do it, it actually has effects!

Like many people, I was drawn to Buddhism because of the promise of meditation. I wanted a way of quieting my thoughts, of accessing inner peace. And I was drawn to the possibility of bringing my mind to its full potential. I must have already known, even as a college student reading Buddhist verse for the first time, how easy it was to get in my own way.

This personal discovery of Buddhism was very important to me. It led me from meditation into a greater exploration of the Buddha's teachings. I came to appreciate that meditation, while important, was not the be-all and end-all of the Buddhist path. The point of meditation was to bring its lessons to everyday life: to be able to live more fully in the moment, to stop undermining myself, to be less afraid of myself and others, to be less at the mercy of my impulses, and to give more generously in the midst of a busy and demanding day. In my years of work as a psychiatrist, I have come to see that these can also be goals of psychotherapy.

Until recently, I have avoided too much direct talk of Buddhism in my therapy. I have tried to bring it in less explicitly: in the way I listen, for example; in the way I ask my patients to approach their own shame and dread; and in my efforts to show people how they are perpetuating their own suffering. I make no secret of my Buddhist leanings and am happy to talk of them when asked, but I rarely have offered up meditation as a direct therapeutic prescription. I have watched as mindfulness has taken hold in the field of mental health as a therapeutic modality in its own right, but I have stayed on the sidelines, wary of what has always seemed to me to be people's exaggerated expectations of this single aspect of Buddhist thought. I have preferred to work in the old-fashioned analytic mode, artificially blinding myself, as Freud liked to put it, in order to focus on the dark spot in front of me. There are much more inexpensive ways to learn about meditation than to pay a psychiatrist's hourly fee, after all.

But what if I am wrong? This thought occurred to me in the middle of my own weeklong silent meditation retreat some years ago. What if I am depriving the people I care about of that which has given me so much help myself? In my efforts to avoid being too prescriptive, was I keeping my patients too much in the dark? What if I were to be more explicit about what I had learned from the dharma, as the Buddha's teachings are called? What would I say? How could I talk to my patients, many of whom were not at all conversant in a Buddhist sensibility? The teachings of the Buddha had helped me enormously. Could I give advice about Buddhism without alienating the people I was trying to aid?

Much of the time, when I do offer advice, it is overtly welcomed but covertly rejected. People appreciate my attempt to help them, but they have many reasons not to do what I suggest. Paradoxically, this has freed me up a little. I worry less about it now because I know that people will not listen if they do not want to. But still, I am aware of how alienating it can be to come across as any kind of an "expert." A patient of mine, sober now for twenty years, told me something recently that confirmed my cautious approach. When he'd first come to see me, he said, back when he was still drinking and using drugs, I'd suggested only once that he go to AA. It was very meaningful for him that I said it only once.

"You let me find it on my own," he told me, and this made it all the more consequential for him.

As my patient implied, the desire to help all too often has untoward consequences. If I had been too insistent on his sobriety, my patient might well have kept on using just to frustrate me.

I have not always been so on point, however. I was recently reminded of another event from the early days of my practice, one in which I offered advice but came across as way too much of an authority. I learned from this experience to be very careful with even well-meaning advice. It can boomerang if the therapeutic relationship is not well established. A young man came to me after his own two-week silent meditation retreat. Rather than becoming calm and peaceful on the retreat, however, his mind had become anxious and unglued. He was extremely intelligent but his thinking showed faint traces of what psychiatrists call "thought disorder," signs of an incipient process not necessarily visible to a layperson. I met this young man for a single session, in consultation, because his parents trusted me, as someone knowledgeable about Buddhism, to help their son. As well intentioned as I might have been, I was abrupt in my response to him. I was tired at the end of my day and spoke more impulsively, because of my fatigue, than I should have, or would have ordinarily, I hope.

"You might have an underlying bipolar illness," I told him, "surfacing under the spell of the retreat. It would be good to treat this right away rather than let it impact your whole life."

I remember pulling literature about manic-depressive illness off my shelf and showing it to him, explaining that if you had to have one psychiatric illness, this was the one to have because there were such good treatments for it and it did not have to wreck your life.

"Lots of very accomplished creative people have it," I told him reassuringly.

The evidence to support my intervention was slim—this man functioned well enough in his regular life and had come apart only in the silence and sensory deprivation of the retreat—but this did not stop me. My advice did not go over well. He was offended, and he left. The next day his mother called me, and she was furious.

"How can you make that diagnosis based on one visit?" she lambasted me.

She was right. I apologized but never heard from them again.

Twenty years later, I ran into this patient's mother at a party. She came over to me and reminded me—unnecessarily—of what had happened all those years ago.

"You have children now, right?" she asked me. "You know how devastating it can be to hear that anything is wrong with them? I was mad at you for a long time."

I knew exactly what she was saying. I apologized again and asked how her son was.

"Well," she said, "I told him I was going to see you tonight. 'He could have been right, Mom,' he told me. He's had more trouble on those retreats since then, but he's starting to come to terms with it now."

Might I have been able to help this person if I had come across as less of an expert all those years ago? Even if I was right (and I was secretly glad to know that I had not been completely off base), being right is not the point in this profession. Being useful is. I do not want any advice I am offering to be as counterproductive as this session had turned out to be!

This book is my attempt to be useful. Its advice can be used by anyone—each in his or her own way. As the Buddha made clear in his own advice on the matter, the Eightfold Path is there to be cultivated. Just as no artist makes work identical to any other, no person's development will look or feel the same as anyone else's. We are all coming from different places and we all have our own individual work to do, but it is safe to say that a willingness to engage with the principles of the Eightfold Path will, at the very least, give wise counsel in a confusing world. As hesitant as I have been to offer meditation as the solution to anyone's problems, rethinking the Eightfold Path has allowed a Buddhist perspective to merge with my psychotherapeutic one. The bottom line is this: The ego needs all the help it can get. We can all benefit from getting over ourselves.

One

RIGHT VIEW

Not long after the meditation retreat in which I questioned my advice not given, several of my patients, independently, asked if I would teach them to meditate. I was a bit taken aback by the synchronicity of it all. At least three people in rapid succession made the request. Each wanted to spend a fraction of their therapeutic hour in contemplation and each wanted me to guide them through it. I was happy to comply, although I did wonder if they were trying to avoid telling me something. But I decided to take their requests at face value and give it my best. In offering them meditation instruction, however, I found that it was necessary to speak clearly about Right View. Otherwise, it was too tempting for my patients to turn meditation into just another thing they were failing at.

Meditation is deceptively simple. There is really nothing to do. We sit still and know we are sitting. The mind wanders off and when we catch it wandering we use it as a reminder to continue paying attention. Right View asks us to remember why we are attempting such a peculiar thing. Much of our lives is spent thinking about the future or ruminating about the past, but this dislocation from the present contributes to an ongoing estrangement and a resulting sense of unease. When we are busy trying to manage our lives, our focus on past and future removes us from all we really have, which is the here and now. The Buddha had the rather paradoxical insight that it is difficult to remain comfortably in the moment because we are afraid of uncertainty and change. The present is not static, after all; it is constantly in motion and we can never be absolutely certain about what the next instant will bring. Past and future preoccupy us because we are trying to control things, while being in the present necessitates openness to the unexpected. Rather than resisting change by dwelling in the relative safety of our routine thoughts, as we tend to do in our regular lives, when meditating we practice going with the flow. We surrender to impermanence when we meditate. Wherever it may lead.

If we are doing concentration meditation, we try to restrict the attention to a single object like the breath. When the mind wanders, and we notice it wandering, we bring awareness back to the breath without berating ourselves. If we are doing mindfulness meditation, we try to be aware of things as they shift. When we are sitting, we know we are sitting, but when we are thinking we are aware of that, too. We might notice the sensations of the breath or the physical sensations of the body or the feelings of the mind or the act of thinking itself. The mind jumps around and we follow where it goes. Or we try. When it gets out of control, when we are lost in thought or caught up in emotion and unable to be mindfully aware, there is always an instant when we realize we are not paying attention. At that moment, we bring ourselves back to something simple like the breath and begin again.

Over time, the mind becomes accustomed to this way of paying attention. It learns how to settle back and accommodate. Leaving itself alone, it nevertheless stays present with whatever is going on as it is changing. And a kind of clarity emerges. Like adjusting a radio dial, you know when the signal is right. The mind tunes in to its own frequency and begins to resonate. For a long time there is only distraction, but then suddenly, with no warning, it shifts and things come into focus. It is something like those *Where's Waldo?* books we looked at with our children when they were young. Waldo, in his red-and-white-striped shirt, Dr. Seuss hat, and glasses, is camouflaged in densely illustrated crowds that are spread out across two big pages. At first, it is impossible to find him: there is simply too much going on. But gradually, one learns to relax one's gaze and the figures begin to emerge. Out of all the cacophony, suddenly—there's Waldo!

Like looking at the picture book, meditation can be focused or it can be relaxed. It is even capable of being both at the same time. The mind can be at one with itself, humming along, soft, clear, and deep, and also able to catch a sudden movement: a bird's wing in flight, an internal craving, the rustle of the wind, or the specific features of a character like Waldo. The mind is capable of so much. When we put it into a neutral gear, as happens in meditation, it does not shut down; it opens. It relaxes into itself while somehow maintaining its subjectivity, its critical ability, and its independence. Meditation is training in looking to the mind. Sometimes, inexplicably, it settles down quickly and makes meditation seem easy, but at other times it refuses to cooperate and gives umpteen reasons why the whole effort seems ridiculous. We have to both trust and mistrust the mind, often at the same time. This takes practice.

None of my three patients felt they were doing it right. One wanted to know how long to do it for, as if the length of time were the important thing. She had heard that twenty minutes twice a day was the minimum to get a good effect. She was sure she couldn't sit still for more than five minutes, so I told her five minutes was fine and we figured out how to set the timer on her iPhone so she would not have to peek at the clock. Another person felt defeated by how tense her neck felt. She wanted the relaxation benefits right away, the stress reduction, and she was frustrated when the meditation did not provide it. She felt her tension more acutely when meditating and became convinced she was a bad meditator. Although I told her there was no such thing as a bad meditator, I do not think she believed me. The third person dropped into a peaceful and quiet state initially and then could not reproduce it in the following sessions. She saw no value in periods that were not of the sublime character she had first tasted and began to disparage herself. I was familiar with all of these reactions, having had them myself, and worked as patiently as I could to counter my patients' newfound convictions. I wanted the meditation experience to support, not to erode, their self-esteem.

In thinking about my patients' requests in light of these experiences, I began to understand one reason for my long-standing reluctance to introduce meditation directly into therapy. People often hope that meditation will be the answer to their problems. They look to it as a kind of home improvement project, as a way of fixing a broken aspect of themselves. They let their regrets about the past and their hopes for the future condition their approach to the present moment. In therapy, we have developed ways of countering these kinds of unrealistic expectations. Therapy is hard work and the payoff does not come immediately. Therapists guard against promising too much and become skilled at showing people how their hopes for a magical cure can obstruct their investigation of themselves. Many people become frustrated with the slow pace of therapy and leave. But those who stay are rewarded by what can become a deep and meaningful relationship. People do not have to pretend to be other than who they are in therapy. They do not have to apologize for themselves but can be honest and revealing in an ongoing way. This can be a great gift and is at the heart of what turns out to be therapeutic for many people.

Right View was the Buddha's way of proposing something similar, his way of encouraging people to be realistic about themselves and the nature of things. Right View asks us to focus on the incontrovertible truth of impermanence rather than trying to shore up a flawed and insecure self. Turning meditation into another thing to strive for is counterproductive. Setting up too concrete a goal for oneself—even a worthwhile goal, such as to be more relaxed, less stressed, more peaceful, less attached, more happy, less reactive—is to subvert the purpose of the meditative process.

When the Buddha taught Right View, he was trying to help with the most painful aspects of life. The microcosm echoes the macrocosm, he said. When we observe the moment-to-moment nature of our experience, the way it is constantly changing, we are also seeing a reflection of the transience and uncertainty of the greater whole. In this world, there is no escaping old age, illness, and death; no way to avoid eventual separation from those we love; and no way of insulating ourselves from time's arrows. Right View is a kind of inoculation against these inevitabilities, a way of preparing the mind by using its own intelligence so that it does not need to defend itself in the usual ways. The Buddha found that a simple acknowledgment of the reality of things could help life become more bearable. Acknowledging impermanence is a paradoxical injunction; it is counter to most of our instinctive habits. Ordinarily, we look away. We do not want to see death, we resist change, and we pull ourselves away from the traumatic undercurrents of life. We use what therapists call "dissociation" to protect ourselves. In dissociation the ego pushes away that which threatens to undo it. We banish what we cannot handle and soldier on as if we are not as fragile as we actually are.

But the Buddha was like a contemporary behaviorist who teaches people to carefully go toward the things they fear the most. What we face in meditation is a mini version, or a magnified version, of what we do not want to face in life. A brief experiment with meditation can make this clear. Try closing your eyes. Let your attention go where it chooses. Make no effort to direct it. Most likely, before too long, you will find yourself lost in thought. Pay attention to what those thoughts are, though, even if this is difficult. It is rare that we are having new and important thoughts; most often we are just repeating things to ourselves we already know. What will we do later? What will we have to eat next? What tasks do we have to take care of? Who are we angry with now? Who has hurt our feelings lately? We just repeat these thoughts endlessly, with a minimum of variation. All too often, the present moment slips away from us without our even noticing. We are divorced from it, just as we are separated much of the time from our own bodies. We live primarily in a disembodied mental universe, interrupted periodically—these days—by a need to check our phones to see if we have any messages. As in touch as we might want to be with others, we are very practiced at being at a slight remove from ourselves. But if we try to counter these habitual tendencies, the mind's ability to drop its defensive and dissociated posture can be a real surprise.

Meditation begins by asking us to rest our minds in our bodies, as we rest our bodies on a cushion or in a comfortable chair, and to pay deliberate attention to, rather than ignore, the shifting sensations of the physical organism. These sensations can be subtle, but by spending time with them we start to see two important things. First, the inner experience is changing incessantly. When we are lost in thought, we are protected from this knowledge, but when we dislodge ourselves from our usual mental preoccupations we cannot help but see. Second, it becomes clear how easily we are driven out of the present moment by our own likes and dislikes. When something uncomfortable happens, we move away. When something pleasurable comes, we try to enhance it. We do not let the moments pass easily; we are subconsciously engaged in an endless tug-of-war with the way things are.

To get a sense of how meditation works with this, close your eyes again. Just listen to whatever surrounds you. Sound is a good object of meditation because we generally do not try to control it as much as we do other things. People often have a more difficult time settling into their bodies than they do paying attention to the sounds that appear naturally. Just listen and try to let whatever sounds are around pass through you. Listen in 360 degrees, to the sounds and to the silences that interrupt them. Notice when your mind identifies the sound as a car or a baby or a bird or the television, when the concept of what is making the sound replaces the actual physical sensation of the sound striking your eardrum. Notice when you like something and when you do not and how this changes the way you listen. We tend to move away from a continuous direct experience of our senses into a mental reaction to, or representation of, them. This is one of the things Right View is meant to illuminate. In our day-to-day lives, this shortcut is a big help. If someone honks his horn at us, we don't listen to its sound waves rise and fall; we react and look to see what the problem is. As helpful as this involuntary reaction can be, we use it more than is necessary. It is as if we are constantly on guard. Right View asks us to explore this in the relative calm of meditation. When we see how much it drives us in the micro universe, we get some sense of how it might be conditioning us in the macro one.

Each new loss, each disappointment, each unanticipated difficulty presents a new challenge. The Buddha made Right View the first branch of the Eightfold Path in order to remind us that a willingness to engage with such challenges is the most important thing of all. The aging of our parents, the deaths of our pets, and the travails of our children or other loved ones often feel like more than we can bear. These days, even getting from one place to another can seem overwhelming. The line through airport security takes forever; the plane sits on the runway while the cabin temperature rises or the flight is inexplicably canceled. And when you finally do arrive at your destination, someone's luggage is lost. Daily life is filled with such obstructions. Things break. People hurt our feelings. Ticks carry Lyme disease. Friends get sick and even die.

"They're shooting at our regiment now," a sixty-year-old friend of mine said the other day as he recounted the various illnesses of his closest acquaintances. "We're the ones coming over the next hill."

He was right, but the uncertain underpinnings of life are not specific to any single generation. The first day of school and the first day in an assisted living facility are remarkably similar. Separation and loss touch everyone.

The Eightfold Path begins with Right View in order to address this at the outset. There is a famous saying in Tibetan Buddhism that a person who tries to meditate without a clear idea of its purpose is like a blind man wandering about in open country with no idea of which direction to go. Right View states that the fundamental purpose of Buddhist meditation is not to create a comfortable hiding place for oneself; it is to acquaint the mind, on a moment-to-moment basis, with impermanence. When the Dalai Lama told the Nepalese hermit to get a life after his years of solitary contemplation, he was invoking this very principle. Enter the flow, he was saying; don't pretend you are above it all. While meditation *can* be used to temporarily quiet the mind, from the perspective of the Eightfold Path this is done in the service of a keener and more pronounced observation, not as an end in itself. Just as it is hard to watch a movie in a noisy room where people are talking all of the time, it is difficult to pay attention to the shifting flux of experience when we are distracted by thought. Concentration meditations, in centering the attention on a single object like the breath, still the mind. But mindfulness emphasizes impermanence.

When the mind is settled, the underlying ephemeral nature of things can be more clearly perceived. Resistance diminishes, the flight to past and future recedes, and the sense that it might be possible to respond consciously rather than react blindly to events begins to emerge.

My patients' attraction to meditation and their subsequent difficulties with it have something to do with the way it has been marketed in our culture and something to do with human psychology. Promoted as a method of stress reduction, as a means of evoking the relaxation response, lowering blood pressure, countering the fight-or-flight response, and increasing cognitive efficiency, meditation has entered Western culture as a practical tool to help people cope. Increasingly, it is being offered not only as an adjunct to psychotherapy, but as a replacement for it. In my view, this is unfortunate. Unfortunate in the same way an overenthusiasm for Prozac was unfortunate. People want there to be a magic bullet. They want something quick and easy that will work. When Prozac first became available, a lot of people who did not need it took it, hoping that it would change them. It helped some people enormously and an enormous number of people not at all. But the placebo effect is very powerful. When people are invested in the possibility of a cure, they will convince themselves, at least for a while, that things are better.

From a public relations point of view, meditation has benefited from this tendency, but I am suspicious of this. As I have experienced on many retreats, nice things can happen when you meditate. Peaceful feelings *can* emerge. They do emerge. A concentrated mind is a quiet mind in which the pressures of having to be somebody recede. Artists, writers, mathematicians, chess players, ac-

tors, musicians, and athletes, to name a few, know this very well.
The self disappears when the mind is concentrated, and there is
genuine, if temporary, relief when this happens. In meditation, the
feelings of flow that are common in creative pursuits can be ac-
cessed, harnessed, and stabilized, sometimes for extended periods
of time. But most artists, writers, mathematicians, chess players,
actors, musicians, and athletes are no happier, and no more together, than the rest of humanity. If the temporary dissolution of
self were all that was needed, problems would not be so tenacious.
Even watching television would be therapeutic.

My wife is a sculptor who understands the joy that immersion
in creative process can bring. She spends long and laborious
hours in her studio but generally emerges enlivened and clear.
Through her, I have met and worked with numerous artists whose
experiences in their studios, where the sense of self is temporarily
suspended under the spell of one's creative pursuits, parallel what
can happen in meditation. But working with these artists has reinforced my sense that familiarity with flow, by itself, is not ordinarily enough to help with the deepest challenges life throws at us.
Something akin to the Buddha's Right View is also needed.

Arlene and I had a very meaningful demonstration of this a
couple of years after we were married. We were visiting with
Joseph Goldstein, one of my earliest Buddhist teachers, whom she
did not yet know very well. Arlene received a piece of advice from
Joseph that day that had a huge impact on her. It was not meditation advice per se, but it did seem to contain the essence of Right
View. We both remember the interaction vividly, although when

we saw Joseph recently and reminded him of it he seemed to have no recollection of it at all. In fact, he seemed slightly surprised, even sheepish, to hear what he had told her.

"That was very bold of me," he said with some embarrassment, after she recounted the story to him.

Shortly after our first child was born, in the mid-1980s, Arlene's best friend from art school was diagnosed with cancer. Her friend was an amazing person: brilliant, energetic, ambitious, and full of life. She and my wife shared a spacious loft in downtown Boston for several years after graduating from the Rhode Island School of Design and she was the maid of honor at our wedding. When we moved to New York, she remained in Boston, and when she got sick my wife traveled back and forth to see her as much as she possibly could. Her physicians at first thought she had ovarian cancer, but when the tumors failed to respond to any of the standard treatments, they investigated further and changed their diagnosis to a cancer of the connective tissue called a leiomyosarcoma, a rare, mysterious, aggressive, and, in this case, fatal disease.

Arlene was terribly upset when she spoke with Joseph. The news had gone from bad to worse, to worse than she could possibly imagine, and it was hard for her to hold the twin realities of our infant daughter's aliveness and her friend's illness. We did not see Joseph often, but she had gotten to know him a little and she knew how much I trusted him. Joseph and I had already been friends for twelve years. I had met him while I was still in college and first interested in Buddhism. He had just returned from seven years in India and I was one of his first students in the West. I had traveled with him in Asia to meet his Buddhist teachers there and had done a number of silent retreats under his auspices. I am sure this bond made the subsequent conversation possible. Joseph was like family to me and this must have put both of them at ease with each other. Arlene tearfully explained the situation to him.

"Stop making such a big deal out of it," he replied upon hearing her sorrowful account. "Life is like this. Like fireworks." He gestured with one hand as if to mimic the fleeting nature of things. "Vibrant and alive," he continued, "and then gone."

Arlene felt what Joseph was saying very deeply. There was warmth to his words that may not come through on the page. He was being realistic; he wasn't being unkind, nor was he coddling her; and she appreciated it. But he was also giving her very specific advice.

"Don't make such a big deal out of it."

I am not sure she had ever considered that as a possibility.

I can see why Joseph seemed taken aback when reminded of this. Were I not to know the circumstances of the conversation so intimately, and the parties involved so well, I might think that Joseph sounded callous or my wife naive. But I can attest to the impact his advice had on her, as well as to her lack of naiveté. The conversation came at just the right moment and was given with all the care, confrontation, and clarification that the best psychotherapists seek to cultivate when offering counsel to their patients. Joseph helped Arlene at a very difficult moment in a way that has had a lasting effect on both her life and her work. But his words were nothing I could ever imagine saying to a patient or a friend. Talk about advice not given! Yet, somehow, Joseph must have felt that Arlene could handle it. She remains grateful to him to this day.

There are various ways to understand what Joseph was trying to communicate and why it was so helpful. From one perspective, he was simply being a Buddhist teacher and pointing out the inevitability of change. One of the most fundamental principles of Buddhism, after all, is that impermanence is the inescapable flavor of worldly life. In using the metaphor of the fireworks, Joseph was undoubtedly evoking the Buddha's fire sermon, one of the first that he gave after his enlightenment, in which he famously declared, "Everything is burning," capturing the reality of transience in one devastating image. My wife understood the Buddhist reference, but she was touched on more than a conceptual level. Her mind was engaged by Joseph's admonition and she took the ball and ran with it.

"When he said that," she said later, "I realized he was completely right. Everybody is going to die—don't be too dramatic about it. I had come to the realization, for the first time, that *I* was going to die, which should have been no surprise but *was* a huge surprise inside of me. So to honor my friend, I basically threw out everything in my studio and started anew. Instead of being one of those New Yorkers saying, 'I don't have enough time,' I said, 'Whatever time I have is exactly the time I need!'"

Arlene did not take umbrage at Joseph's comment; she understood intuitively what he was getting at. She had been doing something extra with her grief that threatened to become an obstruction rather than a pure expression of her pain. The story was taking over, as stories tend to do, but she did not have to be its vehicle. She realized there was something more important for her to do in the light of her friend's impending death than just reacting to its horror. In remembering it twenty-five years later, when describing to a museum curator how her work had changed as a result, she put it like this:

"It shook me and woke me up. 'Get used to it,' he was saying. Death is part of life, a reality for me and everybody else. I was gripped by the need to pay attention, to do everything as an embrace of life, and to be alive in every possible way. I was already vulnerable and raw and I saw that celebrating life meant including full-on sadness along with the exhilaration of being alive."

Her friend died in 1990 at the age of thirty-seven, and Arlene, feeling she owed it to her, resolved to live and work more fearlessly. She had just given birth to our second child, and she began to work in a different way in her studio. With two small children, she did not have much personal time, but she resolved to use the time she had gratefully. Out of the simplest of materials, wet plaster and skins of paint, she sculpted works that, much to her surprise, began to resemble Buddhas. It was as if her resolve to live more in the moment were taking direct physical form, without her intending it to. She had never made figurative or iconic work before and she was somewhat embarrassed by it, at least at first.

"I could work with plaster in a short amount of time, and it was riveting. One day I was making something blobby and it looked, I thought amusedly, like a Buddha. In a different state of mind it would have looked like a pile of shit. Despite the fact that I had never had interest in making representational work, suddenly it made sense to use this as a sign of my resolve to embrace aliveness. I became aware that having the physical presence of an icon functioned as a reminder to stay awake, in the broadest way one could use that word. Having the Buddhas in my studio became a source of comfort."

Why should Joseph's comment have affected Arlene so deeply? And what was there in his Buddhist sensibility that led him to make such a blatant intervention? As his reticence all those years later plainly indicated, it is not as if he is in the habit of saying such things to people in the grip of their most intense grief. But there was an opening between them, an opening for a direct communication about Right View. Joseph was not criticizing Arlene for making a big deal out of her friend's illness. It *was* a big deal. But my wife saw that, in her attachment to the story, in her dramatization of the unfairness of her friend's illness, she was resisting a bigger truth. Death is a fact of life. We hide from it, not only by avoiding it, but also by making too big a deal out of it. Right View was the Buddha's method of describing a realistic way of responding to the truth of impermanence. Arlene's embrace of life, and the need she felt to pay attention to each moment of it as a result, was her spontaneous response to, and expression of, this wisdom.

In talking with my three patients about their beginning attempts at meditation, I thought back to this pivotal encounter between Joseph and Arlene. He had managed to show her that there was another way to approach her grief than she had thought. I wanted to do something similar for my patients as they approached meditation. I was struck by how each of my patients wanted to be meditating the "right" way and how each of them considered their own way to be "wrong." In thinking about how to help them, this notion of "right" and "wrong" rose urgently to the surface. The Eightfold

Path advises that certain "right" qualities can be cultivated. When talking about "Right this" and "Right that," however, Buddhism does not mean to imply that all other approaches to life are mistaken. The word "right" means something to us that the original term (*sammā*) did not mean. When we hear "right," we automatically think "wrong." But the word, as the Buddha used it, had other primary connotations. Some translators use "realistic" to convey its sense; others use "complete." To my mind, "right" means balanced, attuned, or fitting. When something is twisted, we set it right. If it is crooked, we right it. The Eightfold Path "is not a recipe for a pious Buddhist existence in which you do everything right and get nothing wrong," says one contemporary Buddhist commentator; it is a means of orienting yourself so that your fears and habits do not tip the balance of your existence.

It would have been inappropriate to try to speak to my patients the way Joseph spoke with Arlene—I try to be watchful of my desires to imitate my teachers—but I did think of two vignettes to relate to them. One came from a serendipitous conversation with someone I barely knew twenty-five years into my exploration of Buddhism. The other came from my college days when I was first learning about meditation in the context of two-week silent retreats. They each clarified something for me about the beauty and utility of the concept of Right View and asked me to give up a preconceived notion of what a "good" Buddhist might look like and of how a "real" Buddhist might act. I wanted my patients to have the same freedom in approaching their meditations as these encounters had afforded me.

The first event happened when I was traveling in the Midwest on a book tour about fifteen years ago. A young woman from a local Buddhist organization met me at the airport. While driving me into town, she told me about something that had been bothering her for a long time, something that had shaken her faith in the dharma. An important teacher of hers had come to stay with her after completing a three-year Buddhist retreat. He was a very accomplished man, a longtime student of Buddhism, and a respected professional in his own right who had made the study of Buddhism his first priority in his later years. While at the retreat, unbeknownst to him, he had come down with colon cancer. He had ignored his mild symptoms until the retreat was over, but by that time the cancer had spread and when he came to live with his former student he was suddenly close to death. She took care of him through his final weeks and was there with him when he died. His last words, on his deathbed, had surprised and frightened her, though.

"No, no, no. Help, help," he had cried.

Wasn't meditation meant to be preparation for death? Weren't you supposed to be able to accept change and die peacefully? Wasn't that the whole point of the Eightfold Path and of his three-year retreat? The young woman took her teacher's fear to mean that his Buddhist studies had been to no avail.

"Was the whole thing a waste?" she wanted to know.

I have thought of this many times in the years that have since passed. The young woman's expectations were certainly in line with Joseph's conversation with Arlene. Death need not be a surprise, and one of the main fruits of meditation practice is to familiarize us with the inevitability of change and the uncertainty of the next moment. But this man, familiar as he was with meditation, was still expressing fear. Perhaps he was just being honest as he faced his final moments. Who says death is not scary, even for someone skilled in meditation? I always think the closest thing to death is birth, and having seen several births, I can definitely say that, as amazing as it can be, it is also very frightening. I have come to believe that this man was modeling something for his friend, showing her that there are no rules when it comes to facing death. The Buddha's agenda for Right View—to face impermanence—extends all the way to the moment of death, and all we can do is to be with it without pretense. I find, when I think of this story, that it does not diminish my own faith; in fact, it gives me comfort.

"No, no, no. Help, help," is a different mantra from the ones Buddhist teachers usually propose, but it is one I can relate to, one that strikes me as universal. To look death in the face and respond truthfully may be the best we can do.

One of the things I have always appreciated about the Buddhism I have known is the way it has urged me to circumvent my own expectations about what an "enlightened" response might be in any given situation. This suggestion runs counter to my own ingrained habits of striving. That is probably why I find the above story so satisfying. Do I have to be worrying for my whole life about how I will be at the moment of death? Will someone be grading me on how I do? Or can I take what I have learned about facing change and let myself deal with it as best as I can? Do I have to be putting on a false front even at the moment of death? Or can I trust myself not to? I could feel how my patients, in their initial attempts at meditation, were held back by their own particular versions of this striving. Wanting to do it for the right amount of time, wanting to make the tension disappear, and wanting to have

the next meditation be as good as the last one all represented different versions of it. My patients' wishes to "do it right" reminded
me of how I felt after one of the earliest silent retreats I ever did.
This was the second vignette I relayed to them.

The retreat was in the countryside north of Mendocino, California, and was taught by Joseph Goldstein and Jack Kornfield,
another of my earliest teachers. I had met both of them at Naropa
Institute in Boulder, Colorado, during the summer between my
junior and senior years of college and was quite enamored of them.
I was twenty-one years old and awash in the exhilaration of discovering a discipline, and a community, that made sense to me.
Joseph and Jack were probably both just thirty years old. There
was enough of an age difference between us at that point to make
them seem like real elders, however, although when I look back at
it now it is hard to believe how young we all were. The two weeks
of silent reflection took place at an old camp in a wooded land-
scape studded with waterfalls and sun-soaked flat rocks perfect
for sunbathing after quick dips in the roaring stream. I was visiting California for the express purpose of the retreat, and when it
was over I got a ride back to San Francisco with Joseph and Jack. I
did not yet know them well and it felt special to be in their com-
pany. We stopped in Mendocino for lunch before making the long
drive. The food at the retreat had been fine, all that I expected,
vegetarian with an emphasis on inexpensive grains that could feed
the hundred participants, but we were hungry. I was ready to embrace a vegetarian diet if that was what was called for and was
mostly focused on becoming an accepted part of this new group.

Much to my surprise, Jack Kornfield ordered a hamburger.
I did a double take. A hamburger? After a retreat? A Buddhist

teacher? I felt suddenly lighter. I was ready to superimpose a set of expectations on myself that went all the way down to what I could have for lunch. Right View, Right Speech, Right Livelihood, Right Action, and Right Lunch.

I did not even want a hamburger. But if I did, I could decide for myself. I have always been grateful to Kornfield for this moment— one I am sure he has long forgotten, one that solidified my sense of Right View. The lesson I took from it was that my Buddhist leanings did not mean I had to cloak myself in a false identity. Even as I was pursuing Buddhism, I could be myself. This left me free to investigate more easily. The Eightfold Path was relevant just as I was, no matter what my diet was or how I might act at the time of death. It was offered in a way that encouraged me to figure things out for myself. I did not have to let my expectations rule my experience and I did not have to follow anyone blindly. I might be wandering in open country, but I had a sense of direction. This path, as Right View made clear, was designed to help me be real with myself.

Two

RIGHT MOTIVATION

Right Motivation suggests that we do not have to be at the mercy of our neuroses if we do not want to be. The conscious mind, when properly oriented, can, with practice, rise above the conditioning of its subconscious influences and intentionally direct a person's activity. More often than not, as therapists know all too well, we are run by impulses we cannot see. Habitual and repetitive patterns of reactivity dominate the untrained mind. Buddhism, practical as always, takes this as a given, but says it is only a starting place. We can shake free of our unconscious influences if we first admit they are there, if we can find and identify them, over and over again, as they appear in our day-to-day lives. Right Motivation encourages us to come out from our hiding places, to use our powers of observation for our own good, and to be real with ourselves. It is the branch of the Eightfold Path that brings conscious intention to the forefront—that asks us to use our intelligence to our advantage, and to not let our fears and habits determine the direction of our behavior.

A friend of mine, a Buddhist psychotherapist named Jack Engler, has a story about his understanding of Right Motivation that has long stayed with me. Almost forty years ago, Jack traveled to the village in India where the Buddha was enlightened to study with the Bengali teacher who had taught Joseph Goldstein about Buddhism. Joseph had spent seven years in conversation with this man; Jack felt fortunate to be able to be with him for several months. He had gotten a Fulbright fellowship after completing his clinical psychology doctorate to, among other things, assess the psychological health of South Asian masters, but his primary motivation in journeying to Bodh Gaya was to learn meditation from this man. Much to his consternation, however, Munindra, the teacher, talked to him of nothing but the health of his bowels for several weeks. Was he constipated, did he have diarrhea, had he tried the various remedies available in the local market? I have since learned that this is an acceptable way of making preliminary conversation in the culture Munindra was part of—much like our talking of the weather—but for Jack it was incredibly frustrating. After two weeks of it, he finally confronted Munindra during a walk in the fields behind the Chinese temple.

"When are you going to teach me the dharma?" he asked, unable to mask his exasperation any longer.

Munindra gave Jack an answer that he immediately felt might be profound but which, at the time, he could not really deal with. Only after mulling it over after his return to the States did its wisdom begin to sink in.

"The dharma?" Munindra replied, feigning surprise at Jack's sudden impatience. "You want to know about the dharma? The dharma means living the life fully."

I am fond of this vignette for several reasons. For two weeks, Munindra was intent on giving Jack no advice whatsoever. Finally, when pressed, he blurted out the counsel he had not been giving, simple words that took on special meaning for Jack because of the relative silence that had preceded them. In his unwillingness to make the practice of meditation the sine qua non of Buddhist wisdom, Munindra echoed the admonishment (to get a life) the Dalai Lama gave to his ascetic follower. And like Joseph's advice to Arlene to not make such a big deal out of her friend's illness, Munindra's message was the kind of general—even simplistic—statement that I have trouble imagining being made by a Western therapist, even though living the life fully is probably the real goal of psychotherapy, too. Jack had made a long and arduous trip to India wanting meditation training, but Munindra did not play directly into his agenda. To my mind, he wanted Jack to have a bigger picture before he started watching his breath. He wanted him to know what the real purpose of meditation was. What did it mean to live the life fully? What stops us? From the Buddhist perspective, what stops us is our ego's selfish—or we might say neurotic—motivation.

Munindra was offering Jack a window into Right Motivation, not by telling him to be more altruistic, nor by telling him to meditate with the intention of liberating all sentient beings (as is often the case in Buddhist communities), but by encouraging him, in his offhanded way, to examine how he was *not* living his life fully. By not cooperating with Jack's expectations for meditation training,

Munindra was performing a classic Buddhist function. Pulling the rug out from underneath his student, he gave Jack a motivation he has always remembered.

Right Motivation, which is sometimes rendered as Right Intention, Right Thought, or Right Understanding, at its heart concerns the conscious resolve to shape one's life based on Right View. Munindra was reminding Jack of this. It can be tempting to use meditation to resist change rather than opening oneself to the ceaseless flow we are made of. It can be tempting to use it to avoid looking at oneself rather than to investigate one's deepest habits and fears. Many people practice meditation to escape from themselves, to replace a life they are estranged from with a more restricted, contained, and manageable one, lived primarily on the meditation cushion. Munindra did not want Jack to fall into that trap. In psychoanalytic language, he did not want him to be stuck in the anal stage, where control is the big issue and obsessive-compulsive routines originate. Munindra wanted Jack to question the agenda he had for himself, to examine his motivation, even if that meant not getting what he had come for. For there is a risk involved in Right Motivation: the risk of surprise—the risk of consciously reaching for something outside of our comfort zone; the risk of staying present with ourselves but letting go of habit and routine, even if that means coming clean about where we are stuck.

Right Motivation did not come easily to me either. It was one thing to understand the words and quite another to put them into practice in my life. I saw this most vividly in the early years of

my marriage when, despite seven or eight years of regular meditation practice, I found myself vulnerable to intense emotions I
could not understand.

While I was outwardly happier than I had ever been, my psyche was in turmoil in those first years of marriage. I began to have
trouble sleeping and became uncharacteristically demanding of
my new wife's affections in the middle of the night. Needing her
sleep, Arlene was gentle but firm with her boundaries. She knew
she could not fix the problem for me. I tried to use meditation to
calm myself but was distraught and confused at what was happening. Buddhist practice, by itself, was not enough to clarify what
was going on with me; I needed the help of a therapist. This was
important for me to see. It gave me renewed respect for the importance of psychotherapy and added to my caution about presenting
Buddhism as a complete treatment for anyone's psychological ills.

When I did manage to sleep, I dreamed recurrently that my
teeth were clenching against themselves so hard they began to
crumble. I would wake from these dreams in fright, afraid that I
was actually hurting myself, and wary of dropping back into sleep.
It is possible that meditation was helping me to be more conversant
or, as John Cage had once indicated, more fluent with the information coming in through my senses and up through my dreams, but
I did not know what to make of what was happening. The dreams
persisted and began to evolve. I would be trying to get through to
someone on the telephone—calling my wife, for example—but as I
dialed the phone it, too, would start to crumble. Then my teeth
would start in. The crushing feelings were intolerable and I would
wake with another start. I brought all this to my therapist.

"Oral rage," he said right away, spelling out for me something I had read about but never thought could actually apply to me.

Oral rage is the anger that children exhibit in the earliest years of life—when the mouth is the primary erogenous zone and the breast or bottle the most important source of connection. Nourishment and comfort are one and the same in this "oral" stage of psychosexual development, and an infant expects (if an infant can be said to "expect") that their needs will be met immediately by whoever is taking care of them. Children in these years, around the time when their teeth first come in, exhibit intense fury when they are not immediately gratified. They attack their parents with the full force of both love and hate when they are in need. Young children do not have words for these feelings. There is not enough of what is called "secondary process" in the mind—the ability to think symbolically or abstractly about something—for the child to understand what is going on inside of them in these moments and there is certainly no ability to postpone the immediacy of their demands. In many cases, parents are able to respond in a timely manner, with enough sympathy and care, so that the anger gets pacified or diffused. The child is reassured and his or her rage becomes manageable. But sometimes, for myriads of reasons, the response does not come, or does not come in time. In such situations, rage becomes unmanageable. Situations in later life that evoke a longed-for intimacy can make it erupt once again.

As my therapist and I talked, my dreams coalesced into an actual memory. I was four or five years old and my parents had left me to babysit for my younger sister, two years my junior, while they went next door to play bridge with their friends. I was a responsible child, even at that age, and my parents had entrusted me to watch over my sister while she napped. There was an intercom connecting the two houses—I still remember it—and they gave me instructions on how to call if I needed them. My sister had cried and I had been anxious after they left. The memory of the intercom came as I was describing one of those dreams in which the telephone disintegrated.

I was able to give meaning to my perplexing sleeplessness through all of this. The happiness of my marriage had made separation challenging. I was hungry for the connection and deeply uncomfortable when it was absent. It echoed that earlier time of my life when my wish to be the responsible child had created conflict with my need for contact. Perhaps it even reached back further, into infancy and early childhood, when the first inevitable separations and frustrations take place. There was no way of knowing for sure, but there was enough of an explanation in all of this to settle me down. I was turning separation into abandonment and acting as if there were no tomorrow. On one level, I was having insomnia. On another, I was experiencing separation anxiety. But my dreams were showing me something even deeper. There was a primitive anger underneath my anxiety that I was not in touch with but that was driving my behavior. Therapy helped me to acknowledge this anger, to make a place for it, and to give it understanding. The dreams went away, and while my insomnia still rears its head on occasion, I am now able to use meditation for what it is good for. It does help contain those primitive feelings when they rise in the night, even if it could not help me understand where they came from or make them go away.

My breakthrough in therapy aided me immensely in my marriage but did not free me as much as I might have wished. I was still vulnerable to my early conditioning even if I had a better understanding of its roots. In fact, one of my first attempts to bring Buddhism directly into my work was compromised for just this reason. Driven by an unacknowledged fear, I acted in a way that undercut the message I was endeavoring to communicate. In retrospect, my behavior seems related to the issues I was facing in my marriage, although at the time these connections were not at all clear to me.

I was teaching in the mid-1980s at the New York Open Center, a clearinghouse in downtown New York City for all things New Age, with two old friends. In those days, the Open Center was on Spring Street in Soho; I believe it had opened just a short time before. I had recently completed my residency in psychiatry and begun to see private patients, and my friends invited me to join them in leading the class. I had done very little of this kind of thing yet and was still young and finding my way. This was not long after Joseph's pivotal conversation with Arlene, and I was hopeful, empowered by my friends, that I, too, would be able to help people better understand the dharma. We called our workshop "Clinical Relaxation," and we planned to offer meditation to people who were looking for new ways of dealing with stress. But I was anxious in my new role. I have a vivid memory of trying to calm myself in the upstairs bathroom of the Open Center that morning, my intestines churning and unresponsive to my internal pleas. I could have used a conversation with Munindra myself on that day to help me deal with such things.

The morning session went well enough—we talked about stress and gave preliminary instructions in concentration and mindfulness—but at lunch my friends told me they had to catch a train at four forty-five that afternoon. Something important had come up, and even though the workshop was scheduled to run until five p.m., they would have to leave early to make it to the station in time. I would have to run the last hour by myself.

I remember how startled I was when they told me.

"What?" I exclaimed to myself. "You're leaving early? What? What about me?"

Maybe it would have been easier if they had asked me nicely, I thought, if they had not just laid it on me as if it were a fait accompli. But this is the kind of thing I often find myself thinking when I am angry or hurt. If only so-and-so hadn't said it *that* way, if only they had asked me in a different manner. . . . The fact was, I was pissed. But I was not prepared to deal with it with them. What was I going to do?

My mind worked very fast. "Okay. If they are leaving, I'm going to leave, too," I thought. "No way I'm going to be left holding the bag."

Looking back at this many years later, I find it hard to fathom why their early departure was so threatening. What was the big deal about running the class for an hour by myself? In subsequent years I have come to be comfortable in these kinds of situations, but in those days it felt like a challenge I was not necessarily up to. In thinking about it, I can see that my reaction was as much about being abandoned by my friends as it was about the unexpected opportunity of leading the class by myself. Rather than dealing with it in any sort of straightforward way, however, I tried to turn it into a teaching for the participants. I remember thinking what an elegant solution I had come up with.

My idea was the following. Our day was structured with periods of silent meditation alternating with lectures and discussions. At the end of the afternoon, just before my friends were to catch their train, we would begin a period of extended meditation. People would be sitting quietly with their eyes closed, watching their breath, practicing Right Mindfulness. While everyone was sitting, we would just slip out the door. Sooner or later people would grow restless, open their eyes, see that we were gone, and know that the day was finished. There was the possibility of a huge spiritual lesson. What did they need teachers for? Wasn't Buddha-nature inside them already? They were looking to us as some kind of authority, but their wisdom was already within. Just as Munindra had refused to buy into Jack Engler's need for meditation instruction, so could we challenge our students' expectations about us. They wanted us to make them feel better, but they had to do it for themselves. The best advice we could give them was no advice at all!

My friends did not object to my plan. It is quite likely that it did not exactly register with them. They had to make their train, they had another engagement, and they had decided to hand responsibility over to me. That I was not really taking responsibility eluded them, as it eluded me. I was pleased with myself, and while I was not unaware of my lingering anger, I did not yet recognize how I was acting out my insecurities by inflicting the same kind of abandonment on our students that I was myself trying to avoid. While my friends let their early departure be known to the group, my plan did not include any warning to the people in the class that I would also be leaving early. I was just going to disappear. A rather creative demonstration of the Buddhist notion of no-self, I thought.

All went smoothly with my scheme. I introduced the final meditation, my friends left for their train, the group sat there in silence together with their eyes closed, and I quietly got up and tiptoed out of the room. I did not think about it much thereafter—the workshop was over for me and I was on to the next thing. A week went by before the Open Center forwarded me a stream of vituperative letters from participants who were hurt by my abandonment of them. There was no e-mail in those days, so it took some time for the consequences of my decision to catch up to me.

"Where was the compassion in your action?" they wanted to know. "What were you thinking?"

In teaching the Eightfold Path, Buddhism often stresses the balance necessary between wisdom and compassion. Compassion without wisdom is sometimes called "idiot compassion" and manifests as someone giving too much and destroying himself or herself along with whomever they are trying to save. It is common in abusive relationships where the afflicted partner keeps on forgiving the abusive spouse, or in situations where a person is addicted to something and another person—a parent, spouse, or child—enables their loved one's addiction by being overly forgiving. But there can also be wisdom without compassion. I am not sure that my little teaching exercise qualified as wisdom, but it was certainly lacking in compassion. My motivation was not Right Motivation. It was motivation based in fear and insecurity, not in regard for the other. As befits the connectivity of the Eightfold Path, the untoward consequences of this failure of motivation had a ripple effect. Saying nothing of my plan was not Right Speech. Leaving my students to fend for themselves was not Right Action. The effort to avoid my anxiety was not Right Effort. Tiptoeing out of the Open Center was not Right Livelihood. Forcing my students to be attentive while being abandoned was not Right Mindfulness. And disappearing was not Right Concentration.

My failure at the Open Center helped me in an unforeseen way, however. It made me aware that my personal life was not as disconnected from my spiritual life as I might have expected, and that issues that were bedeviling me on the home front could unexpectedly show up elsewhere. This led to a change in my understanding of Buddhism and reinforced for me how important it was going to be to integrate what I was facing in my own life with my Buddhist leanings. If Right Motivation means living the life fully, then therapy has an important role to play.

Right around this time, I published a piece about Buddhism in a classical and widely read British journal of psychoanalysis and I received letters from three respected New York analysts after the paper was published. Each of the analysts independently suggested that I read the work of a British child analyst named Donald Winnicott, whose work centered on the notion of the "good enough mother" and on the transitional objects of childhood—the blankets or stuffed animals that help children navigate separation. Something in my depiction of Buddhism had evoked Winnicott for each of them. I was only vaguely familiar with his work at the time but I was intrigued and began to read him. He was especially attuned to the kinds of things I was discovering in myself: the primitive emotional experiences of children before the onset of language. Among many brilliant and provocative insights was one that my own issues had alerted me to. Because children are filled with emotions they cannot understand, they are completely dependent on the people around them to "hold" their emotions for them and make those feelings bearable and, later, intelligible. Parents do this instinctively by comforting their children when they are upset and letting them know that things will be okay. Winnicott wrote of how inevitable failures in this "holding" leave scars. When there is a "good enough" environment, children develop a faith that emotional experience is manageable. When there is not, there is a sense of being "infinitely dropped."

In my article, written without knowledge of Winnicott's work, I had taken issue with Freud's well-known depiction of mystical experience as a return to the "oceanic feeling" of the infant at the breast. But I had said that Freud was nevertheless onto something. While I did not use the phrase "holding environment," I tried to describe how meditation creates a container in which otherwise uncomfortable feelings can be known and investigated. The meditator does not have to regress to infantile narcissism, as Freud had imagined, for the unprocessed emotions of childhood to be revealed; they come up naturally—sometimes when meditating, sometimes in dreams, and sometimes, as in my case, in love. What I found so helpful in Winnicott's work was that he had explanations for where these feelings originate. His explanations supported what I had discovered in my own therapy; his approach dovetailed with my therapist's and reinforced the insights my teeth-crushing dreams had given me. Rather than treating my uncomfortable feelings solely as annoying obstacles, I was able to investigate them, think about them, and use them to come to a more compassionate understanding of myself.

My efforts to integrate Buddhism with therapy shifted during the subsequent few years. I saw how relevant Winnicott's way of thinking was for my patients, as well as for myself, and I strove to make my office a place where people felt safe enough, over time, to reveal the feelings that frightened them, the ones they did not understand and that threatened their grown-up equilibriums. My focus became increasingly centered on therapy; I felt it was important to offer people the opportunity to work with their primitive emotions from a psychodynamic perspective.

It was not until two other friends from my Buddhist circles moved to New York City and invited me to teach with them that I made another attempt to bring the two worlds together. Robert Thurman is a professor of Tibetan Buddhism at Columbia University and one of the first Westerners to ordain as a Buddhist monk in the school of Tibetan Buddhism headed by the Dalai Lama. And Sharon Salzberg is a meditation teacher in the *vipassana* tradition of Theravada Buddhism, the Buddhism prevalent in Sri Lanka, Myanmar, and Thailand. She is one of the founders of the Insight Meditation Society in Barre, Massachusetts, where I have done the majority of my silent retreats. The three of us have now taught together for almost twenty years. As our teaching has evolved, I have found myself elaborating many of the themes of this book. Rather than presenting meditation as a technique of stress reduc-

tion, with Bob and Sharon I always began by discussing the troubling feelings I had discovered in myself. I had spent enough time
as a therapist by then to realize that I was not alone in grappling
with such issues and that many people who were coming to learn
about Buddhism were also struggling to understand their deeper
and more frightening impulses. Buddhism by itself does not easily
address the kinds of things that psychotherapy takes as its bread
and butter, and that Winnicott wrote about so evocatively. In order
to make Buddhism relevant in today's world, where our psychological selves are part and parcel of what we bring to meditation, I
found it very useful to explain Winnicott's perspective and to talk
about the value of psychotherapy. Buddhism has a lot to offer, but
it needs help with the kinds of psychological issues that we often
face: issues of relationships, of childhood, and of emotional reactivity rooted in an unresolved past.

When teaching with Bob and Sharon, I almost always began
with a famous paper of Winnicott's, called "Hate in the Counter-
Transference," which compares a therapist's frustration with his or
her patients to that of a mother who cannot help but sometimes hate
her beloved infant. I love presenting the paper to people interested
in meditation because it helps to make anger a worthwhile subject
of inquiry rather than simply a disturbing element they are trying
to get rid of. Winnicott's paper has a sinister undertone, a realistic
appraisal of the human condition, combined with an uplifting, almost spiritual message, unusual in a professional discourse.

In his paper, Winnicott invokes eighteen reasons why
mothers hate their infants. He does not do this with any kind of
malice, judgment, or condescension, but with an empathy and
humor born of experience and understanding. To my mind, his

main point is that rage, of the kind I experienced in my dreams, does not magically disappear (even when there has been a "good enough" childhood) but manifests in adult life whenever frustrations are encountered, even in situations, like parenthood, where we might rather pretend it does not exist. His thesis is that therapists, in order to help patients with their issues around anger, must be comfortable with their own deepest feelings, just as a mother, in order to help her child navigate his or her own destructive urges, must be comfortable with her own. "However much he loves his patients he cannot avoid hating them and fearing them," he writes, "and the better he knows this the less will hate and fear be the motives determining what he does to his patients." In reflecting on my behavior at the Open Center, I could see how relevant this warning could be!

My favorite passage from the paper comes toward the end:

> A mother has to be able to tolerate hating her baby without doing anything about it. She cannot express it to him. . . . The most remarkable thing about a mother is her ability to be hurt so much by her baby and to hate so much without paying the child out, and her ability to wait for rewards that may or may not come at a later date. Perhaps she is helped by some of the nursery rhymes she sings, which her baby enjoys but fortunately does not understand?
>
> *Rockabye Baby, on the tree top,*
> *When the wind blows the cradle will rock,*

When the bough breaks the cradle will fall,
Down will come baby, cradle and all.

I think of a mother (or father) playing with a small infant: the infant enjoying the play and not knowing that the parent is expressing hate in the words, perhaps in terms of birth symbolism. This is not a sentimental rhyme. Sentimentality is useless for parents, as it contains a denial of hate, and sentimentality in a mother is no good at all from the infant's point of view.

It seems to me doubtful whether a human child as he develops is capable of tolerating the full extent of his own hate in a sentimental environment. He needs hate to hate.

This image of a mother or father singing to their baby about their own ambivalence has always moved me. It speaks to the real experience of the parent, to the endless demands a new baby puts on one, and to the satisfaction that emerges when one's own selfish motivations are both acknowledged and restrained. The most re-markable thing about a mother, to paraphrase Winnicott, is her capacity to take it all personally without taking it personally. His description of the parental state of mind is true for the meditative one as well. It does not need to be a blank slate or an empty void. There can be tenderness but also humor, self-pity mixed with self-deprecation, anger swaddled in love, a teasing quality that is nevertheless subservient to the rocking, singing, and cradling of the lullaby. And behind it all, there is the echo of the inevitability of separation and change as described by Right View: *Down will come baby, cradle and all.*

Talking about such things to a Buddhist audience always gives me a certain thrill. It is not what they are expecting. In recruiting Winnicott to embellish Buddhism, I am not only extolling the power of meditation to mimic the mind of a good enough mother, I am also emphasizing how psychotherapy has something important to teach us about how to evoke this essential mind-set. While I have made much use of this in my teaching over the years, I have also found it immensely helpful in my clinical work.

One of my most spiritually accomplished patients, for example, a gifted woman named Claire who had practiced meditation for more than twenty years, consistently came up against the feeling that she was not real to me, that I cared about her because it was my job but not because she actually meant something to me. This is not an unusual feeling in therapy but it was very persistent with Claire. For a long time I could not figure out how to work with this feeling. If I were to be too reassuring, I might miss the deeper meaning of her insecurity, but if I were to ignore it, I would be missing something essential.

As I got to know Claire, I found that she often seemed more comfortable with her meditative attainments than she did with her own history. She tended to use meditation as a doorway to an empty and infinite expanse into which she could dissolve. She liked to go to this place in her imagination and hang out there. It gave her a sense of peace but also a feeling of sadness. There was a desolate quality to it that I could feel whenever she spoke of it. For Claire, meditation was an alternative to everyday reality; it was a place she could go to get away from things that bothered her. Once a day, or more often if she was angry or upset, Claire liked to smoke a cigarette. The way she talked about the cigarette and the way she spoke of meditation were similar. Both offered respite from the daily grind, a retreat from all that aggravated her. In my therapy with her, I often thought back to Munindra's comment about living the life fully. Claire's persistent feeling of not mattering to me was an important clue about what was holding her back, but I did not quite understand the connection.

A breakthrough came one day when our conversation circled around to Claire's father. We were able to tie together several significant events in her life while making sense of the feelings therapy was bringing up. Claire's father had left the family when she was two years old. He had remarried and had another child and come to visit when she was thirteen. She remembered seeing him playing on the living room carpet with her two-year-old half brother and feeling that the scene was too "obscene" to look at. "Obscene" was her word; it startled me when she said it and I asked her to explain. It was too rich, she said; it seemed like the perfect father-child moment, the kind of thing she had always longed for in life, and she had to look away. While there was more sadness than rage in Claire's voice as she relayed the scene, it was clear to both of us that a deep anger underlay her experience. Claire's own needs for her father's attention must have also seemed obscene to her at that time. How could she not have felt there was something lacking in her? Was she still harboring this feeling within?

Several years after this vision of her father, Claire became anorexic. She would spend her evenings looking at pictures of food in magazines, salivating over the images, after having surreptitiously thrown her own dinner in the garbage. Sometimes she played a game. She would look at herself in the mirror to check whether she was real. The longer she looked, the more dissociated she would become. After a while, she did not recognize the stranger's face in the mirror and she would pinch her skin, touching her face again and again to check whether she still held any physical reality. When I suggested that she must have wondered whether she mattered to anyone, she rejected that idea. The question was not, "Did she matter?," she told me; it was, "Was she still matter?" What Claire felt lacking was the right to have needs at all.

When her mother belatedly realized what was happening, she plied Claire with candy and desserts until her appetite returned. While this would never be sanctioned in the therapy world as an effective treatment for anorexia, it worked for Claire. She could not resist the lure of the sweets, or the reality of her mother offering them to her, and she began to eat again. I am sure her mother was operating purely on instinct but she managed to turn her daughter around. She accomplished something therapists have a notoriously difficult time doing in the treatment of anorexia: she restored a normal appetite to her. But her unconscious wish to dematerialize did not go away.

When Claire began to practice meditation in her late twenties, she had an intense but frightening experience. Unlike many people who begin to meditate, she found it very easy to do. Her thoughts did not preoccupy her and she settled into a tranquil and peaceful state. Feelings of joy and bliss arose, and she went with them easily. But all of a sudden she became afraid. She felt separate from her body and did not know how to get back to it. Her heart began to beat furiously, but she was locked into a disembodied state. It quickly lost its blissful character and became a kind of dissociated panic from which she could not leave. It was not until one of her teachers sat with her, eyes open, breathing in and out while staring into her eyes, that she was able to come back to her day-to-day mind and body.

The richness of the interpersonal world remained something Claire felt unworthy of despite the best efforts of her mother and her meditation teacher. Her basic premise, disguised in her veneration of meditation, was that she was not real. She felt it in her relationship with me, and it is fair to say it had become an unconscious pillar of her identity. Claire's ego was convinced of its own insignificance. It was a big deal when she could find the right words to express this and a bigger deal when she saw where her convictions were coming from and began to take my regard for her seriously. Claire often said, as she got better, that instead of "cornering" her with my understanding, I "welcomed" her in our sessions. I made room for her uncomfortable feelings in a way that allowed her to make room for them too. Until then, her feelings of unreality—and the needs and emotions hidden beneath them—were outside of her awareness but conditioning a good deal of her behavior. Claire's therapy allowed her to take possession of her history, painful though much of it had been. In turning away from the sight of her father, she had also turned away from herself. There were important feelings she was trying to avoid at the time, feelings that then seemed as obscene as the love on display in front of her. Those feelings—of longing, envy, anger, and self-doubt—could now start to be integrated. Right Motivation, in my view, led in this direction.

Emotions still have a bad name in many Buddhist circles. When I was learning meditation, the emotions I was taught about most often were the obstacles, or hindrances, to meditative stability that are known to all those who try to quiet their minds. These hindrances are usually listed as anger, lust, worry, doubt, and fatigue, although "fatigue" is given the more arcane name of "sloth and torpor." *Who* is it that is angry? *Who* is it that lusts? the Buddhist teacher wants to know. Behind each of these feelings is a sense of an all-important "me"—a person, striving to exert control, at the center of a mostly uncooperative universe. This way of working with the emotions, while incredibly useful at certain points, tends to leapfrog over the important and meaningful personal content bound up with such discomfort. Claire's therapy is a good example of this. She wanted to avoid her uncomfortable feelings by whatever means possible, but this left her feeling unreal. Emotional content needs a welcoming attitude; otherwise it will remain undigested, waiting to jump out at inopportune times.

There is a tendency among Buddhist practitioners, and even among many Buddhist teachers, to lump all feelings together and to see the spiritual path as one in which "toxic" aspects of the self, like the emotions, are "cleansed" through practice. Through the eradication of such "defilements," it is assumed, a state of quiescence can be reached, a state of calm defined by the absence of emotional disturbances. Claire's view was very close to this one. It is reminiscent, in the language used to describe it, of the dynamics of toilet training associated with the Freudian anal stage, where the cleansing of one's waste in the service of order and control is also emphasized. This way of practicing leads to a kind of paralysis, however. Rather than opening up the underlying flow of feelings that marks our connection to this world and makes us human, there is only retreat and routine. In the guise of openness, emotions are shut down. Feelings are pushed away. A kind of joylessness masquerades as equanimity.

This is not to suggest that it is not important to learn to detach from difficult feelings in meditation. They are not called hindrances for no reason. But the idea that they must be eradicated is dangerous. In bringing Winnicott into a dialogue with Buddhism, I have endeavored to show an alternative. Right Motivation is the motivation of the ordinary devoted mother. She is not put off by hate but realizes that she has the wisdom and compassion to hold even the most difficult emotional experiences. This capacity is inherent in the good enough parent. Winnicott made it clear that this is the best model for psychotherapy. It seems to me that it is also needed in Buddhism. Let us treat the primitive emotions of childhood as motivation for growth rather than as obstructions to be eliminated. Treating emotional life as an obstacle is an obstacle in itself. One's personal history cannot be erased, after all.

Three

RIGHT SPEECH

While Right Speech conventionally means abstaining from lying, gossip, vain talk, and hurtful rejoinders—all of which create turmoil in the mind—it has taken on an additional meaning for me. How we talk to ourselves is as important as how we speak to others. The way we think is as crucial as what we say out loud. Both Buddhism and psychotherapy ask us to pay careful attention to the stories we repeat under our breaths. We tend to take them for granted but they do not always accurately reflect the truth.

Right Speech is traditionally presented as the first of three ethical qualities to be cultivated on the Eightfold Path. Right Action and Right Livelihood are the subsequent two. Outer speech is emphasized because there is a choice involved in what we say and how we say it. It is rare, even when we are trying to free-associate, that we actually speak without thinking, without some kind of intentionality behind what we say. The classic approach to Right Speech asks us to pay attention to the space between thought and action and to intervene when the words we want to say have a toxic quality. It asks us to abstain from language that serves no good purpose, from words that are hurtful or distracting. But we do not ordinarily experience the same kind of choice in our inner lives. Our private thoughts seem to happen by themselves. Repetitive and destructive patterns of thinking drag us into circular eddies of criticism and blame, often with our self, or those close to us, as the target.

While the classical portrait focuses on refraining from harsh outer speech, in my view Right Speech can also be applied in our inner worlds. We can catch and question our loops of thought and rein them in, interrupting what appears to be an involuntary inner cascade. Many people are resigned to the way they speak to themselves. They do not like it yet they accept it as a given. "This is just who I am," they say when pressed. But resignation is not the form of acceptance that Buddhism recommends. Right Speech asks us to take seriously the stories we tell ourselves, but not to take them for granted. Seeing them clearly gives us back some power over them. "Just because you think it," I often say to my patients, "doesn't make it true."

Meditation is like looking at this under a microscope. An itch comes and we tell ourselves we have to scratch it *or else*. Our back hurts and we think we can't take it anymore so we had better get up and move. We are stuck in traffic and get agitated about how late we are going to be and arrive in a frazzled state, having already imagined the worst. Something breaks and we rush to assign fault rather than dealing with the situation carefully or intelligently.

Meditation suggests that we stay with the raw material of a given experience longer than we are used to—whether it is the itch, the pain, the delay, or the sudden loss—and to question our secondary add-ons. In emotional terms, my tendency to turn separation into abandonment is a good example of this. Separation is difficult for me, but when I give it the added meaning of abandonment, it starts to seem impossible.

When people who have never meditated are first introduced to it, they are often surprised by how easily their thinking hijacks them. Beginning meditation involves learning to stay in the body, following one's physical sensations as they rise and fall over time. But Right Speech, in my interpretation, is a reminder not to remain stuck in the body. How we talk to ourselves continues to matter. This becomes very clear when it comes to observing one's emotions. The raw feeling of the emotion is one thing and the mental component, in which we attach meaning to the feeling, is another. It is rare that we bother to separate the two.

For me to make sense of the feelings I encountered in the first years of my marriage, I needed to find someone I could talk to about them. The feelings had too deep a hold for me to make sense of them by myself and they were too entrenched for me to be able to simply let go of them meditatively. My dreams were talking to me in the night, but I needed to talk about them in the daytime in order to understand what might be going on. Talking about them allowed me to change the story I was telling myself. My knee-jerk reaction was to blame my wife for not being attentive enough in my distress. Once I began to explore this conclusion, however, instead of acting it out, my story began to change. I saw that there was something I had to do for myself that she could not do for me, some way I had to take responsibility for feelings that were beyond my comprehension. In a similar vein, in my work as a therapist, I cannot help people if they do not first tell me, to the best of their ability, what they are thinking and feeling, even if the content is shameful or embarrassing. Simply to dismiss one's thoughts is to miss the boat. One's story never changes if it is simply ignored; it just lies in wait, ready to return with a vengeance.

In my efforts to bridge the gap between psychotherapy and Buddhism by looking at how the emotions of childhood can haunt us in adult life, I found an unexpected and powerful ally in Sharon Salzberg. I met Sharon in 1974 at the Naropa Institute and knew her for more than twenty years before we began working together in earnest. She never intended to become a Buddhist instructor, but slowly and inexorably, with the encouragement of teachers she'd met in India while still in college, she has become one of the foremost proponents of Buddhism in the West. When she moved to New York City at the end of the 1990s, I used to send patients who asked me about meditation to her weekly classes. A number of people went back and forth between Sharon and me, allowing us to collaborate at a distance. As things evolved, when we started teaching together with Robert Thurman and I began to bring Winnicott into the mix of our public discussions, Sharon noticed how someone in our workshops would always ask me to elaborate on what being a "good enough" parent actually meant.

"It means being able to survive one's child's rage," I would answer.

"And what does it mean to survive the rage?" they would ask.

"Not to be invasive and not to be rejecting," I would say. "To be able to hold their anger and be open to their experience without abandoning them but without retaliating either."

Sharon understood that I was applying mindfulness to emotional experience, not just to the physical sensations of the body or the breath. Although I did not know it at the time, despite having been her friend for years, Sharon had a special reason to be attuned to this way of working. She had suffered terribly in her childhood and had worked very hard, with the help of Buddhist teachers she'd met before I knew her, to deal with the negative self-image her suffering had engendered. In 2001, she published a book called *Faith* in which she courageously revealed the many losses of her childhood and described how Buddhism had helped her in their wake. Her book had a profound effect on me. Right Speech was emphasized from the beginning.

"Each of us tells ourselves some kind of story about who we are and what our life is about," Sharon wrote in the first sentence of the book. "The story I told myself for years was that I didn't deserve to be happy. Throughout my childhood I believed that something must be intrinsically wrong with me because things never seemed to change for the better."

That was putting it mildly. Sharon's history was difficult to hear. When she was four, her father disappeared. When she was nine, Sharon had to call an ambulance when her mother, watching TV with her while recovering from minor surgery, started bleeding uncontrollably. Sharon never saw her again; she died two weeks later in the hospital. When Sharon was eleven, her grandfather, with whom she had gone to live, passed away, and her father reappeared. Six weeks after coming home, her father took an overdose of sleeping pills and spent the rest of his life in the mental health system, never to return. Sharon lived with her grandmother until going away to college at the age of sixteen.

She was eloquent in her book about the consequences. One of the most difficult things, she said, was that no one spoke openly about all of the losses she'd endured. There was "an ambient, opaque silence" in the place of any real discussion. This is by no means rare. Patients I have seen whose parents committed suicide or died of illness when they were young almost uniformly report that no one ever spoke of it around them. Sharon described how her feelings of grief, loss, anger, confusion, and despair had to be hidden from the people in her life and from herself.

"The story I was telling myself was that what I felt didn't matter anyway," she wrote. "I didn't care about anything, or so I hoped it seemed. I came to know very well the protection of distance, of a narrow, compressed world. Though it was my own act of pulling back, I felt forsaken. . . . For years, I hardly spoke. I barely allowed myself a full-blown emotion—no anger, no joy. My whole life was an effort to balance on the edge of what felt like an eroding cliff where I was stranded."

Sharon had the good fortune—after years of misfortune—to find the inspiration in Buddhism to turn herself around. Traveling in India while still in college, she stumbled upon some wonderful Buddhist teachers. She used Buddhism to diminish her attachment to her story and began to, in essence, re-parent herself. She found refuge in the Buddha's affirmation that suffering is an inextricable aspect of life and stopped blaming herself for what she had been through. In the place of the opaque silence that had surrounded her while growing up came a new willingness to face her feelings, not embellishing them but not retreating from them either. And she found faith in the promise that all people—even her!—were capable of happiness. In one of the most poignant parts of *Faith*, she confessed that the phrase she had most identified with before meditating was Lucy's famous retort to Charlie Brown in the *Peanuts* cartoon, "You know what your problem is, Charlie Brown? The problem with you is that you're you." When Charlie Brown plaintively asks what he could do about that, Lucy comes back with her own version of advice not given. "I don't pretend to be able to give advice," she replies. "I merely point out the problem."

When we first started working together, Sharon asked a psychiatrist friend what he considered the most important force for healing in the psychotherapeutic relationship. He ventured that the essential ingredient was love. Freud had once said much the same thing, although the phrase he used was more obscure. "The unobjectionable positive transference," Freud had called it.

Sharon disagreed.

"Just showing up for their appointments," she countered. "That's the fundamental thing."

Sharon's answer impressed me. She had understood something important. When locked into her Charlie Brown story about what was wrong with her, she was locked out of her life. To get back into her life she had to repeatedly face feelings she had worked her whole life to avoid. She saw that the protective distance she had created around herself was holding her back and she made deliberate efforts to, in her words, "participate, engage," and "link up." In order to get off the eroding cliff on which she was stranded, she had to learn to relate to the world differently. Her story about herself gradually changed as a result. Freud had a famous quip about this in the closing line of his paper on the therapeutic relationship. "For when all is said and done," he wrote in 1912, "it is impossible to destroy someone *in absentia* or *in effigie*." A person has to show up before their internal monologues can be unpacked and questioned.

Sharon found special help in India from a Bengali woman named Dipa Ma, who was one of Munindra's closest and most accomplished students. Dipa Ma, married when she was a teenager, had lost two infants, her husband, and her health by the time she was in her early forties. She turned to meditation out of desperation and depression at the age of forty-six; still residing in her unassuming Calcutta apartment in the early 1970s when Sharon met her at Munindra's instigation, she had by then become a skilled sixty-year-old Buddhist teacher. She spent a lot of time with Sharon and predicted, to Sharon's great surprise, that she would be a teacher, too, when she returned to the States in 1974.

"You can do anything you want to do," Dipa Ma told her. "It's only your thought that you can't do it that's holding you back. You should teach because you really understand suffering."

I have taken much inspiration from Sharon's experience. Her willingness to look into herself in meditation the way we do in psychotherapy, showing up for her appointments even though it was painful, affirmed the connection I have made between the two worlds. Troubling emotions are valuable objects of meditation too, just as physical sensations can be. People are often more comfortable treating their emotions as obstacles than they are in cultivating an open, accepting, and inquisitive attitude toward their inner lives. But to treat an emotion as a problem is to remain stuck. Even if it is seen as such, what can be done about it? Can it be eliminated so simply? Pretending to eliminate it just leads to falseness. And treating it as a contaminant only reinforces people's negative inclinations. They use the incontrovertible presence of their emotions as further evidence of their failures, as another reason to beat themselves up.

Such feelings, like the ones Sharon was trying to ward off in her young adulthood, often rise to the surface at inopportune moments and derail us. Right Speech means being willing to loosen the attachment we have to the long-standing explanations we have been giving ourselves about them while facing these emotions head-on. This means accepting discomfort, relaxing into it, breathing through it, and asking ourselves what stories we are telling ourselves about it, rather than simply reacting in a conditioned, and all too often self-flagellating, way. I think Sharon was speaking very personally when she said that the most important thing in psychotherapy is showing up for one's appointments. In therapy, when we show up, we look for feelings, bring them out, and make them the subject of inquiry. We talk emotions over, examine them, wonder about them, and explore around their edges. This willingness to separate the raw material of emotion from the story we have built up around it is a critical aspect of Right Speech. It allows us to speak more gently to ourselves in the face of our most intense suffering, not just in the midst of meditation or in a therapist's office but in real life, in the middle of the night when we lie awake wondering what is wrong with us.

When I first heard Dipa Ma's prediction that Sharon would teach because she really understood suffering, I assumed she meant that because Sharon had suffered so much in her life, she would be a good teacher. It was not until years into working with

Sharon that I began to see the statement differently. I now think that Dipa Ma meant something else. Sharon understood suffering, I believe, because she had investigated it on a granular level: exploring and naming the various components she had previously shied away from while holding her premature conclusions up to meditative scrutiny. Sharon really understood suffering because she had investigated it within herself from every possible angle, rather than rushing, as she had in her youth, to the default position of "the problem with you is you."

While Sharon's childhood was beset by very real and concrete losses, the way she explained things to herself is widespread even among people with no such overtly devastating history. Many people feel inadequate without having had traumas on the order of Sharon's. She could remember the various losses she had to endure. Other people can only infer what might have gone wrong. One of the things I focus on most resolutely is the way people are explaining things to themselves. Therapy works when the discussion one has with one's therapist changes the conversation one has with oneself.

A good example of this comes from a patient named Miranda, a respected professor of French literature who came to therapy several years ago. Miranda was an expert in the work of Samuel Beckett. She had chosen him because of her comfort with his understanding of the bleak underpinnings of human existence. Making him into her intimate companion over a twenty-year period, she took refuge in his genius and in the compassion she felt from him in his writings.

At a critical point in her treatment, Miranda had an episode of acute and inexplicable anxiety. She had gone to a friend's empty painting studio in Greenwich Village early on a springlike Monday morning. It was a beautiful studio—private with a view of a little park resplendent with blossoming trees and colorful flowers—and Miranda was excited to go there to write without being disturbed by her family or neighbors. She liked to read Beckett aloud when she could; it helped her concentrate and gave her a deeper feeling for his work. But this morning she began to feel trapped, an invisible wall holding her at bay. An intense fear came upon her, a recurrent and not entirely unfamiliar feeling but one that had not bothered her in a long while.

Miranda had no idea where her pain came from that day, but she was terribly uncomfortable and could not focus. The serene studio took on a malignant air. She spiraled downward and left, consumed by darkness and dread, and spent much of the day wandering the streets of the city.

When we spoke about it the following day, Miranda had one association. She remembered being sure she was going to die when she was ten years old. Her parents did what they could to convince her otherwise, but she then became certain that *they* were going to die and she could not be comforted. In an effort to make her feel better, her parents took her to her grandparents' house, a place she had always loved, and left her there. But this was the first time she had been left alone with her grandparents. She had loved it at their home because the whole family would always gather together there. Now she was separated from her parents, still convinced that they would die. She woke screaming in the night worried that she would never see them again.

The dominant feeling in Miranda's story was one of loneliness, but it was not the fully felt loneliness of someone who has suffered a concrete loss of a loved one. It was a barely tolerated loneliness, more like my fear of abandonment than Sharon's actual feeling of forsakenness, that felt so intimidating—so frightening, so shameful—that the only solution was to banish the feeling altogether. It had erupted unexpectedly in the painting studio, but it was too intense for Miranda to deal with by herself. She found it humiliating and she was loath to investigate it further. Too scared of the pain, she needed a lot of encouragement to examine it further.

In a bout of self-loathing that came pouring out in our session, Miranda insisted that her true nature was needy, depressed, and worthless. I think it was Miranda's use of the term "true nature" that caught my attention. She was not particularly schooled in Buddhist culture, and I do not know if she was consciously referring to a Buddhist concept, but I felt obligated to disagree with her. I did not think the Buddha would agree that her true nature was worthless, or needy, and I did not agree either. I felt her to be more truly herself when laughing than when feeling empty or hopeless.

"All this self-loathing is extra," I tried to explain. "You are laying it on yourself, repeating the same story over and over again. You think you are being honest with me, showing me the real you. But all you are showing me is your self-hatred. Try just releasing it. Right now. For this moment. You don't know your true nature yet. You haven't even begun to make room for it." I thought of Dipa Ma telling Sharon she could do anything she wanted, that it was only her thoughts that held her back. Miranda was not holding her

difficult feelings the way Dipa Ma would have hoped. There was a
rush to judgment that had led to intensifying mental gyrations. I
wanted Miranda to take responsibility for the way she was talking
to herself, not to give her thoughts a free pass.

This notion was a revelation for Miranda. I backed it up with
some meditation instruction, giving her a concrete way of disiden-
tifying with her repetitive thoughts while listening more deeply to
her mind. Miranda could move away from her self-loathing if she
tried. She did not have to indulge it as she had been doing. Her
true nature did not lie in her suffering, in her story, in her hope-
lessness, or in her need. Her true nature was there to be discovered
if she could just question the way she was speaking to herself.

In making Right Speech relevant for my patients, I am inevi-
tably drawn to this notion. I wanted Miranda to see that she could
be with her feelings without the self-deprecating story she had
created in response to them. Was she the vertiginous vortex of
harmful energy she thought she was, sucking and spewing nega-
tivity and need? Or was she . . . something else? Worn down by my
prodding, or enticed by my faith, she became a little more open.
Temporarily willing to question her low self-esteem, to treat it as a
thought instead of a truth, she looked at me with a sparkle in her
eyes and smiled.

"I can try for this," she said.

In subsequent weeks and months, Miranda faced these feelings again. Still troubled by loneliness, she acknowledged it with a
more relaxed attentiveness, allowing it to rise and fall as it wished.
She noted her fear and accepted her anxiety and did not flee from
the feeling. She treated it as something to be beheld, as theater

in its own right. While she did precious little writing when the loneliness was strong, she made significant headway in the investigation of her inner life. And some kind of lightness emerged in her. If Right Speech meant progress in her writing, she failed. But if it meant changing the way she spoke to herself, she found inklings of success.

In my work with Miranda, I had an unexpected ally in Samuel Beckett. In his most prodigious creative burst, beginning in 1946, Beckett wrote his novels *Molloy* and *Malone Dies* as well as his most famous play, *Waiting for Godot*. He spent most of his time that year alone in his room in Paris writing, leaving only for midnight walks among the bars of his Montparnasse neighborhood. According to his biographer, this all began with an epiphany on the end of a Dublin pier in the midst of a winter storm:

> Amid the howling wind and churning water, he suddenly realized that the "dark he had struggled to keep under" in his life—and in his writing, which had until then failed to find an audience or meet his own aspirations—should, in fact, be the source of his creative inspiration. "I shall always be depressed," Beckett concluded, "but what comforts me is the realization that I can now accept this dark side as the commanding side of my personality. In accepting it, I will make it work for me."

This is the acceptance of someone willing to speak gently to himself in the face of tremendous agony, the acceptance of someone no longer struggling to suppress his darkness. This is something essential to both therapy and Buddhism, something that can be applied not only to the blight of depression but also to the inevitable sadness of grief that is an inextricable part of life. All too often, people react to such feelings in much the same way as Sharon described. The effort to push them away, to return to "normal," leaves an ambient, opaque silence in their wake.

I was given additional insight into this when, talking with my eighty-eight-year-old mother four and a half years after my father died from a brain tumor, I was surprised to hear her questioning herself. "You'd think I would be over it by now," she said, speaking of the pain of losing my father, her husband of almost sixty years. "It's been more than four years, and I'm still upset."

I'm not sure if I became a psychiatrist because my mother liked to talk to me in this way when I was young or if she talks to me this way now because I became a psychiatrist, but I was pleased to be having this conversation with her. Grief needs to be talked about, I thought. When held too privately, it tends to eat away at its own support.

"Trauma never goes away completely," I responded. "It changes perhaps, softens some with time, but never completely goes away. What makes you think you should be over it? I don't think it works that way."

There was a palpable sense of relief as my mother considered my opinion.

"I don't have to feel guilty that I'm not over it?" she asked. "It took ten years after my first husband died," she remembered suddenly, thinking back to her college sweetheart, to his sudden death from a heart condition when she was in her mid-twenties, a few years before she met my father. "I guess I could give myself a break."

I never knew about my mother's first husband until I was playing Scrabble one day when I was ten or eleven and opened her weather-beaten copy of Webster's Dictionary to look up a word. There, on the inside of the front cover, in her handwriting, was her name inscribed in black ink. Only it wasn't her current name (and it wasn't her maiden name)—it was another, unfamiliar name, not Sherrie Epstein but Sherrie Steinbach: an alternative version of my mother at once entirely familiar (in her distinctive hand) and utterly alien.

"What's this?" I remember asking her, holding up the faded blue dictionary, and the story came tumbling out. It was rarely spoken of thereafter, at least until my father died half a century later, at which point my mother began to bring it up, this time of her own volition. I'm not sure that the pain of her first husband's death had ever completely disappeared; it seemed to be surfacing again in the context of my father's death.

I had just finished writing a book about trauma when this conversation took place and I felt a real serendipity to its timing. Trauma is not just the result of major disasters. It does not happen to only some people. An undercurrent of it runs through ordinary life, shot through as it is with the poignancy of impermanence. I like to say that if we are not suffering from post-traumatic stress disorder, we are suffering from pre-traumatic stress disorder. There is no way to be alive without being conscious of the potential for disaster. One way or another, death (and its cousins: old age, illness, accidents, separation, and loss) hangs over all of us. Nobody is immune.

My response to my mother—that trauma never goes away

completely—points to something I have learned through my years as a psychiatrist. In resisting suffering and in defending ourselves from feeling its full impact, we deprive ourselves of its truth. As a therapist, I can testify to how difficult it can be to acknowledge one's distress and to admit one's vulnerability. It is much easier to fall into whatever chronic story we have been telling ourselves than it is to stay with our experience. My mother's knee-jerk reaction, "Shouldn't I be over this by now?" is very common. There is a rush to normal that closes us off, not only to the depth of our own suffering, but also, as a consequence, to the suffering of others.

When disasters strike, we may have an immediate empathic response, but underneath we are often conditioned to believe that "normal" is where we should all be. The victims of the Paris terrorist attacks, the Boston Marathon bombings, or the Orlando nightclub massacre will take years to recover. Soldiers returning from war carry their battlefield experiences within. Can we, as a community, keep these people in our hearts for years? Or will we move on, the way the father of one of my friends expected his five-year-old son—my friend—to move on after his mother killed herself, telling him one morning that she was gone and never mentioning her again?

In 1969, after working with terminally ill patients, the Swiss psychiatrist Elisabeth Kübler-Ross brought the trauma of death out of the closet with the publication of *On Death and Dying*. Her five-stage model of grief—denial, anger, bargaining, depression, and acceptance—was radical at the time. It made death a normal topic of conversation, but had the inadvertent effect of making people feel, as my mother did, that grief was something to do right.

Mourning has no timetable. Grief is not the same for everyone. And it does not necessarily go away. The healthiest way to deal with it is to lean into it, rather than try to keep it at bay. In the attempt to fit in, to be normal, we end up feeling estranged.

I was surprised when my mother mentioned that it had taken her ten years to recover from her first husband's death. That would have made me six or seven, I thought to myself, by the time she began to feel better. My father, while a compassionate physician, had not wanted to deal with my mother's former marriage. When she married him, she gave the photographs of her previous wedding to her sister to hold for her. I never knew about them or thought to ask about them, but after my father died, my mother was suddenly very open about this hidden period in her life. It had been lying in wait, rarely spoken of, for sixty years.

My mother was putting herself under the same pressure in dealing with my father's death as she had when her first husband had died. The earlier loss was conditioning the later one, and the difficulties were only getting compounded. I was glad to be a psychiatrist and grateful for my Buddhist inclinations when speaking with her. I could offer her something beyond the blandishments of the rush to normal.

The willingness to face traumas—be they large, small, primitive, or fresh—is the key to healing from them. They do not disappear in five stages, but maybe they do not need to. As Sharon was reminded in her initial embrace of Buddhism, and as Beckett so gloriously expressed, suffering is an ineradicable aspect of life. We are human as a result of suffering, not in spite of it.

Right Speech, in my interpretation, asks us to pay attention to how we talk to ourselves about this inevitable aspect of life, how we exaggerate its implications. So often, within the privacy of our inner worlds, we take the difficult thing and make it worse. Our own subliminal hate speech coats our experience and gives an added layer of meaning to things that are already difficult enough. Right Speech says this is unnecessary. Self-criticism may still arise—old patterns do not just disappear in an instant—but one's stance in relationship to one's inner critic can change. When one learns to observe the addictive and self-perpetuating nature of many of our thoughts, their dominance diminishes. Right Speech takes the sting out of them by bringing awareness to the fore-ground. Refreshed by this discovery, the mind senses relief. My mother's questioning, "I don't have to feel guilty about this?" is typical of this shift. Her conclusion, "I guess I could give myself a break," describes the freedom that is possible. As a therapist, I have been trained to pay careful attention to the words people use in such utterances. Phrases like my mother's "I guess" often slip in without the person being conscious of it and telegraph hesitancy or doubt. Were my mother my patient, I would push on it a little. I might ask her to repeat her sentence but drop the "I guess," for example, to see if she really could give herself a break. But enough was enough. I held my tongue. Even Right Speech has its limits.

Four

RIGHT ACTION

S amuel Beckett's refusal to be intimidated by his depression was very Buddhist. Rather than directing his energy toward getting rid of his dark side, he found a way to let it inspire him. This is the key connection between Right Speech and Right Action. Both involve mobilizing the power of restraint. Before his revelation, Beckett was like a person new to therapy hoping to get rid of whatever was troubling him. After his realization, he was operating on another level. No longer trying to eliminate a part of himself, and no longer propelled by a false image of perfection, he was able to modify his expectations while probing more deeply into himself, ultimately using his explorations for the purposes of making art.

Right Action classically means not acting destructively. Killing, stealing, hurtful sexual activity, and intoxication "to the point of heedlessness" form the nucleus of the traditional ethical prohibitions. Monks take vows about these kinds of things, and these vows confer a double benefit. They protect the community by instilling a strong and shared moral code, and they protect the individual from the internal disquiet that such actions bring in their wake. Buddhism seeks mental ease. If one's actions create disease, they are obviously counterproductive.

But not acting impulsively is not the same as doing nothing. Think of the difference between eating compulsively and preparing a real meal. In the former, there is a blur that often leaves a feeling of disgust in its wake. Large quantities of food are ingested, but there is often little attention to its taste. In the latter, there is restraint but no lack of activity. Right Action means shopping for the proper ingredients, chopping the vegetables, making the meal, and setting the table. An enormous amount of restraint is required even while there is much to be done. Postponing the ego's need for immediate gratification is the core principle of this aspect of the Eightfold Path.

Psychotherapy is fertile terrain for the deployment of Right Action. Because people come to therapy in all kinds of distress with hope for immediate relief, the burden on the therapist is significant. It is wonderful when there is a pill I can give that will quickly alleviate someone's symptoms, but this is the case only a fraction of the time. When I cannot help someone immediately, I have to wait. I have to stop my anxiety, my need to assist, from interfering with the treatment. Therapy is often a long, slow process that centers on building a trusting relationship. As trust develops, there is more and more room for me to act—or speak or relate—provocatively: in a manner that hopefully upsets my patients' preconceived ideas about their problems. This involves edging people gently into discomfort and away from their fixed, and often exaggerated, notions of what is wrong with them. It involves getting them to question stories they have been telling themselves for a very long time. "Acceptance of not knowing," wrote Winnicott, "produces tremendous relief."

This is one of the most exciting aspects of being a therapist, although there are many countervailing forces within the field that seek to tamp down its improvisational nature and replace it with one that is more circumscribed and operational, in which a therapist follows a prescribed plan of action from the start. Right Action encourages therapists not to let their wishes for cure interfere with the treatment, not to let their professionalism become a defense, but to use the rapport that is possible when people trust each other as a therapeutic tool. It is easy to see how the ethical restraint of Right Action dovetails with this. If a therapist takes sexual advantage of his or her patients, for example, the freedom and trust enabled by the relationship are immediately shut down. But it is not just in such grossly violating ways that therapists can undermine their treatments. If they are too focused on being right, too insistent that their advice be adhered to, they run the risk of short-circuiting the help they are trying to give.

When I am able to use Right Action to capture my patients' interest, there is a potential for change. Old patterns can be exposed and new possibilities can emerge. The history of Buddhism is replete with examples of teachers using such trust to undermine students' restrictive notions of who they are supposed to be. Psychotherapy is not far behind. When we can help people see their repetitive thoughts as *mere* thoughts rather than as true stories, there is a whiff of freedom. Our narratives need not be as sure of themselves as we have led ourselves to believe. The more we examine them in an open way, the less convinced we tend to be about them.

While Right Action can help therapists with their own perfectionism, it can also be extremely useful on the patient side. Above all else, people want to know *what they can do* to feel better. This is, for me, where Right Action is most helpful. Many people who are drawn to Buddhism—and many who come for therapy—think that the answer lies in letting go. "Teach me to let go," they ask. "If I learn to meditate properly, will that help me?" Their most common assumption is that letting go means giving up the thing that is bothering them. If they are angry with someone, they tell themselves to let go of their anger. If they are anxious, they try to let go of their anxiety. If they are having disturbing thoughts, they endeavor to dispatch them. If they are sad and upset with themselves, they try to surrender their unhappy feelings.

But letting go does not mean releasing the thing that is bothering you. Trying to get rid of it only makes it stronger. Letting go has more to do with patience than it does with release. There is a difference in direction, in valence, and in spin from how we commonly think of it. There is a famous phrase in Japanese Buddhism that tries to explain this. "Learn the backward step that turns your light inward to illuminate your self," it suggests. Then "body and mind of themselves will drop away, and your original face will be manifest." This backward step is another way of describing Right Action. You settle into yourself rather than trying to make the troubling thing go away. If anything drops away, it does so by itself. You cannot make it happen directly.

In working with my patients, I have found this basic approach to be extremely helpful. When people come for the first time, it is rare that they can explain exactly what the problem is. Often, they do not know, or if they think they know, it doesn't make complete sense.

"Why, when I see a pretty girl coming down the street, do I have fantasies of strangling her?" one seventy-year-old man asks me, deeply upset at his own mind, tormented by these unwelcome, disturbing, and uninvited thoughts. "Why, when you say something helpful to me, do I have images of sucking your balls?"

Such sentences are not uttered easily; there is much anxiety bound up in these obsessive, uncomfortable, unwanted, and usually unspoken thoughts. Ralph is worried that he will not be able to control his actions, that his impulses will get the better of him, although he has never acted on any of his obsessional thoughts. It is a big deal that these thoughts are being spoken and confessed, but do I know why they are happening? Is there a magic word I can say that will relieve him of his torment and make them go away? I encourage his free associations. Perhaps we can find the childhood links that gave such obsessive thoughts their life. Or perhaps not. Will doing so make things better? Or is there another way?

Although Ralph's symptoms are unusual, his bewilderment about them is not. My second therapist, Isadore From, whom I worked with when I began to see patients privately, seemed to know this very well. He would start every one of our sessions with the phrase "What's with you today, Mark?" I always felt anxious under his gaze, never sure exactly what *was* with me that day, or what was with him! I asked him once about this opening gambit and he told me, in a forthcoming manner, that he began every session that way, not just the ones with me. He liked it better than the conventional "How are you feeling?" or "How are you doing?" Isadore did not like pleasantries. He liked to play the edge, putting me in touch with my anxiety right away if I could handle it. He knew I would have preferred something a little less jarring, but that would have played into my defenses rather than helping me out of them.

Often, people arrive in therapy living a scripted life that has not gone as planned. Slowly and steadily, through the process of talking things out, they may come to a greater, but still limited, understanding of what is stifling them. Conversations with Ralph yielded many tantalizing sources of his symptoms. Maybe he could not tolerate feeling attracted to younger women. Maybe he feared rejection, sought preemptive revenge on good-looking women, and could only express his aggression in an obsessional way. Or maybe his thoughts were rooted in that time forty years earlier when he got stoned with his girlfriend and suddenly, out of nowhere, staring at the thinness and fragility of her neck, imagined choking her and went running out of the room in fear. Maybe feeling attracted, or grateful, made him dependent in a way he found too threatening. He grew up in a tough part of town and was always picked on by gangs of bigger boys. Too much dependency would have made him even more of a target. Did any of this conjecture make him feel better? Possibly. But the conclusions themselves did not help as much as the open-ended collaborative questioning we engaged in together.

The most useful thing I ever said to Ralph was that he was not looking carefully enough at the pretty women he was passing on the street. He was allowed to look discreetly, I said—that's what men do. He was choking himself, strangling his instincts, interrupting his looking, and inhibiting his desire. He did something similar with me too, I pointed out. When I said or did something helpful, for which he felt the stirrings of gratitude, he would disconnect from his feelings with an unwanted sexual thought. The forbidden thought would then become the focus of his attention and he would become preoccupied with trying not to have it again. This became a loop, an obsessional loop that was very difficult to get out of. Trying not to have the thought only made it more pronounced and more threatening.

"What's really going on with you?" I wondered. "You bring me these strangulated bits of frightening thoughts, but that is not the real you.

"Stay more with your actual experience," I would say to him in as many different ways as I could muster. "Your breath, your body, what you are actually seeing and feeling. We don't need to make your symptoms go away; we just need to change the way you relate to them. With less aversion to your thoughts, their hold on you will lessen. You could be less preoccupied and more open to what you are seeing around you."

I think I was onto something with him. Ralph liked my advice and found it helpful. His thoughts of choking women did not entirely go away, but he found the encouragement, and permission, to look at the women he passed on the street to be surprisingly useful. Instead of focusing so much on his unwanted thoughts, he started to look around.

"Where do you want to look?" I remember asking him.

He was bashful at first at mentioning women's breasts. Ralph was the kind of person who did not remember faces, who would not notice if there was a change in the decor of a room, who was not attentive to visual cues. There was a visual world, and, I suspected, an emotional and erotic world, he was not living in. He enjoyed the challenge of discreetly returning to his visual field, to the bodies and faces of the women he passed on the street, even when his thoughts intruded; and he found that, as a result, he spent less time dwelling on his obsessional thoughts when they arose. They would still come, but they did not squeeze the life out of him in quite the same way. He began to see his disturbing thoughts as *mere* thoughts, and not as the last word on his moral fiber.

Some might say that, from a Buddhist perspective, encouraging Ralph's voyeurism was counterproductive. Craving is at the root of suffering, the Buddha taught, and desires are endless. Indulging them keeps us in their grip and traps us in a never-ending cycle of brief satisfactions followed by the relentless pursuit of more. Loosening the grip of the instincts is one of the hallmarks of the Buddhist approach. But in order to loosen their grip, we must first know what they are. Ralph was so at odds with his desires there was no way he could work with them. As he began to relax with himself, however, he came to see that there was more to the male gaze than simple lust. Erotic desire often masks a longing for emotional intimacy. His obsessional response to the genuine moments of connection in my office opened a window onto this. He told me one day that such thoughts also happened when he was watching a sunset. This had always been a mystery to him. There was something so tender and heartbreaking in the sunset, he realized, that his mind jumped away to avoid its poignancy.

There is a famous Zen story that describes an ancient version of therapy with patients like Ralph. It is about Bodhidharma, the man who brought Buddhism from India to China and then spent nine years in a cave staring at a wall. Bodhidharma, a legendary figure who lived in the fifth or sixth century, did not like to be bothered. He lived alone in his cave and stared at the wall all day. When people trekked to his outpost to solicit teachings from him, he sent them away. One man, who went on to become his dharma heir, was particularly persistent. Huike stood obstinately in the snow outside the mouth of the cave and would not leave. Eventually, so it is said, he cut off his left arm and presented it to Bodhidharma as proof of his dedication and sincerity. This part of the story is often used as an example of the tenacity one needs to practice Buddhism successfully. I do not think his effortful striving is the point of the story, however, nor is it a description of Right Action I would support. Bodhidharma's intervention, in fact, helps Huike to let go of his striving.

The heart of the story is as follows:

Huike says to Bodhidharma, when finally given a chance to speak to him directly, "My mind is anxious. Please pacify it."

To which Bodhidharma replies, "Bring me your mind, and I will pacify it."

Huike says, "Although I've sought it, I cannot find it."

Bodhidharma then says, "There, I have pacified your mind."

Huike, in his desire to be freed from his anxiety, was very similar to Ralph. And Bodhidharma, in a paradoxical move, helped him therapeutically. In asking his visitor to find the mind that was

troubling him, Bodhidharma got his attention. In creatively moving Huike out of his comfort zone, away from his fixation on his
anxiety, Bodhidharma was deploying Right Action. He managed to
get Huike to change his focus and acknowledge that the mind he
was convinced was at the root of his problem was not there in the
way he imagined. His non-finding *was* the finding, most Buddhist
teachers insist. The mind's empty, aware nature was there all along,
already pacified. This skillful exchange made Huike aware of it.

There is something of this in a successful psychotherapy. People come with their symptoms, and, while they may not be as
aggressively demanding as Huike, they are essentially asking their
therapists to pacify their minds. If I only had to repeat a Zen story
to them, life would be beautiful. But the challenge is to be as re-
sourceful as Bodhidharma, not to imitate him. He elicited the
story Huike was telling himself and playfully undercut it. He gave
him a different way of understanding himself not by instructing
him, but by making it come alive in their interaction.

This kind of approach is not alien to psychotherapy. There is a
long history of experienced therapists doing whatever they can to
shake their patients out of their comfort—or should we say discomfort—zones. Once when I was teaching a three-day workshop
on Buddhism and psychotherapy, I had a conversation at lunch
with a woman twenty or thirty years my senior who had seen Wilhelm Reich for a consultation when she was in college in the late
1940s. Her encounter with him reminded me of Huike's with
Bodhidharma. For me, hearing her story was akin to meeting
someone who had been in treatment with Sigmund Freud himself.

To hear it in the context of a workshop on Buddhism and therapy was particularly delightful.

Reich was one of Freud's younger disciples. He met Freud in 1919 when he was twenty-two years old and not yet out of medical school. He quickly rose in prominence in the Viennese psychoanalytic circles and developed his own theories of character analysis and the function of the sexual orgasm before becoming increasingly erratic and controversial in his later years. Reich's central idea, for which he was both praised and ridiculed, was "orgastic potency." He was an early precursor of the body-centered therapists who have become much more established in our own time, and in the 1920s he was a teacher of Fritz Perls, the founder of Gestalt therapy, who was therapist to my own Isadore From.

Reich felt that conflicted emotions were stored as muscular tensions and that people's "characters" could be read via these chronic inhibitions. The orgasm, which Freud called Reich's "hobby-horse," was, for Reich, the most critical vehicle of release. Not only could one's muscular tensions dissolve, but the ego itself could temporarily lose its rigidity under the spell of sexual intercourse and the surprise of orgasm. These ideas, while no longer so arcane, were quite controversial in Reich's time. Freud felt that they were something of a one-liner, that both the psyche and neurosis were more complex than Reich envisioned. But Reich's ideas, and his personality, had power, and his influence stretched over several continents.

In 1939, Reich came to New York City and set up an office in Forest Hills, Queens, where he saw patients for the next ten years until he moved permanently to Maine in 1950. The woman in my workshop must have seen him sometime in that interval. She told a table full of people from the workshop her story over lunch, and I am sorry I did not take notes immediately so that I could get the details correct. But I remember the basics. She was returning home from college for a vacation and had some kind of intense anxiety at the train station in New York City that paralyzed her. In today's jargon we would probably say she had a panic attack. She could not go home and could not go back to school, and she must have managed to contact a friend. I cannot remember how, but somehow someone got her to go see Dr. Reich. As he apparently did with all his patients, he asked her first to undress and lie naked on a table in the back room so that he could observe her. She complied. Then he asked her to get dressed and come talk with him in his consulting room in the front of his office suite.

"Your problem," Reich said to her, "is that you don't know how to flirt. I'm going to teach you how."

Reich had her pretend she was on the subway. He was sitting across from her and reading the paper, and she had to make eye contact with him and flirt. They role-played for the better part of the session and something in her gave way. She enjoyed herself and she believed him that her anxiety was a function of her sexual timidity. As an older woman at the weekend workshop sixty years later, she was confident, charismatic, and vivacious. My twenty-year-old son was there at the table and she teased him with gusto as she recounted her tale. She obviously felt that he would be able to relate to her story. Reich's intervention all that time ago had started her on her way. This woman told me this story in the light of connections I was trying to make between therapy and Buddhism. Reich's intervention opened her: to her needs, her desire, her body, her attractiveness, and her capacity to reach others. But his intervention also had a spiritual component in that it helped her reach outside of her ego—outside of her known self. It held out the promise of less isolation and more connection. And it gave her permission as a young woman to assert herself in a manner she must have felt was forbidden.

"Flirtation," writes therapist Michael Vincent Miller, "as a social art form, is a mode of play, specifically, the play of the imagination. It involves two people playing with fantasy together about what could happen between them without either insisting that he or she knows exactly what the other has in mind. Flirting is an absorbing means of making contact, sometimes fleeting, sometimes prolonged, that leaves the mysterious unknowability of the other intact. It is at once provocative and respectful."

Looked at from this perspective, there is a direct parallel with Buddhism. Flirting is an exercise in creating and maintaining uncertainty. Bodhidharma, in asking for the impossible, used flirtation to loosen Huike's anxiety just as Wilhelm Reich did thousands of years later in his office in Forest Hills. While it is not often talked about in such stark terms, psychotherapy, to this day, does not shy away from flirtation's potential to unleash therapeutic change.

Louise Glück, in a poem entitled "The Sword in the Stone," gives a vivid and personal account of just this kind of flirtation. There is none of Bodhidharma's samurai energy in her report, and little of Wilhelm Reich's extravagant role-playing; the poet in this case speaks sparingly from her analyst's couch. Yet the underlying feeling is unmistakably similar.

My analyst looked up briefly.
Naturally I couldn't see him
but I had learned, in our years together,
to intuit these movements. As usual,
he refused to acknowledge
whether or not I was right. My ingenuity versus
his evasiveness: our little game.
At such moments, I felt the analysis
was flourishing: it seemed to bring out in me
a sly vivaciousness I was
inclined to repress. My analyst's
indifference to my performances
was now immensely soothing. An intimacy
had grown up between us
like a forest around a castle.

Glück's description of intimacy as a forest surrounding a castle is very moving. The Buddha, of course, left his castle for the surrounding forest in search of unconstrained freedom. The forest was where he discovered himself, where his ingenuity and exuberance were brought to full flower. It was where he freed his sword from its stone.

I reflected upon this in a series of conversations with an elderly former teacher of mine named Tori. Tori lives in a suburban independent living facility not far from the house she shared with her husband for many years. She has a very nice apartment within this facility, but it is like being in college or living in a monastery.

As beneficial as this place has been, it is not what Tori had in mind for herself. Tori tried to stay in her home after her husband died, but it was too difficult to manage. Against her will, but in line with her children's pleas, she moved outside of her comfort zone. The social aspect of this new living situation has not been easy, however. Married for more than fifty years, Tori now has to navigate a slew of new relationships by herself. She is always pleased when I call or visit, and many of our talks have centered on this unanticipated challenge. Tori is a good sport about it and she has not let her anxiety stop her from reaching out to new people. But she has had to deal with one unexpected event as a result, one that led her to her own understanding of Right Action.

At the peak of her husband's career, he was the dean of the university he had spent his career at. He ran into political problems, though, as happens often in academia, and was forced out of his position as dean. A committee of three people—the vice chancellor of the university, the chairman of the history department, and one other administrator—had recommended that he step down. This was a big disappointment for him and an embarrassment for Tori. Her husband, characteristically, did not say much to anyone about his feelings, but Tori was very hurt and angry. She blamed the vice chancellor in particular for the unceremonious and ungracious way her husband was informed. It had come as a complete surprise. It was as if a storm blew through their lives and left them in the wreckage. Tori's husband stayed on at the university and carved out a respected place for himself, working until he became ill at eighty-one and passed away. He seemed to make his peace with it all, but Tori harbored bitter feelings for both of them.

As chance would have it, Tori's residence was full of elderly professors. The head of that history department lived down the hall when she first took her apartment. And now, a couple of years later, the former vice chancellor moved into the community as well. He was someone Tori and her husband had known well, until they stopped talking in the aftermath of her husband's dismissal. For Tori, this was like a horror movie, the return of the repressed. Here she was, locked into this place, with no way of avoiding the uncomfortable reminder of one of the most painful aspects of her past. Right away, she was asked to a dinner at which he was included.

Dinners at a retirement complex are important social events, much like lunches in high school or suppers in college. Residents make plans to eat with one another. There is a whole etiquette to work out. Those who do not participate socially are left on the margins. They have to eat by themselves or are put at tables with people with incipient dementias. Tori, after chafing against this new reality, had become adept at scheduling her meals with people she liked. Were she to try to avoid the vice chancellor she would suffer socially. Her daughter urged her to swallow her pride.

"Be polite and go to dinner with him," she advised.

Tori agreed, and, much to her relief, the first evening with him went fine. They did not talk beyond exchanging pleasantries, but it felt like a hurdle had been crossed.

The next day, however, while picking up her mail, the vice chancellor came up behind her. His post box was right beneath hers.

"Tori," he said, as she tensed up at the sound of his voice. "I wanted to talk to you about Joe."

It was good of him to say something to her, I thought when I heard the story, good of him to break the ice. Tori had gone to dinner with him and now he was reaching out to speak to her about her husband.

"He was a good man in the wrong job," he said.

They had a conversation there in the mailroom, a conversation that never would have happened but for the coincidence of the two of them ending up in the same residence. Tori was shaken but also relieved. She finally had a chance to say something to this man about what had happened. She told him how unfair it had been to not give Joe more of a chance. His dismissal had come so suddenly; it had been such a shock. There was no warning; her husband had assumed he was doing a decent job.

The vice chancellor was taken aback by Tori's words.

"We had at least three prior conversations about it," he told her. "I told Joe it wasn't going well. There were political problems. He had a real chance to turn it around."

Tori then realized that her husband had kept all this from her. Even after he'd lost the deanship, he did not tell her of the earlier warnings he had received. Tori was disoriented by this information. Her prior version of events—the one that had defined both her and, in her mind, her husband—was now open to question. She had been telling herself this particular story for years, holding the grudge for Joe's sake, but now the story had a big hole in it. Relieved of her explanation, a feeling of humility arose to take its place. I thought she might be angry with her husband for keeping the truth from her, but she seemed to feel only compassion. He had not wanted to let her see his shame.

"A good man in the wrong job," the vice chancellor had said.

She could see his point.

Tori's embrace of the vice chancellor's overture reminds me of a Buddhist story of two monks crossing a river. The two men come upon a young woman who is having trouble getting to the opposite shore. One of the monks, despite his vows to never touch a woman, picks her up and deposits her on the other side of the water. As they continue on their way, the other monk, the one who has kept his vows and not touched her, can't stop chastising his overly benevolent friend.

"How could you do that?" he asks. "You know touching a woman is against our vows. And you were *holding* her."

"I put her down long ago," replies the first monk. "You are still carrying her."

I have always loved this story. The monk who picked up the woman, while breaking his vows, did what was required in the moment. He responded sympathetically to the person in need and exhibited Right Action. The other monk, holier than thou, while adhering to the letter of the law, was the more attached of the two. Playing by the rules, he was looking for safety rather than paying attention to what the situation called for. His unconscious severity was structuring his response and, we can infer, masking his envy of his friend's serendipitous contact with the stranded woman. Even after his friend had put her down, the second monk was still obsessing over her. While endeavoring to be a good Buddhist, he was inadvertently revealing just how difficult it was for him to let go.

Buddhist tales make this point over and over again. Our lives are made dull by our efforts to overcontrol things. The joy of creative expression arises out of surprise. If we live our lives like the overly severe monk thinking only about the rules, we walk through life with blinders on. If we can be open, like the first monk, we find that life's unpredictability is full of interesting and invigorating challenges. These challenges engage us in unexpected and unanticipated ways and allow for the freedom of unscripted responsiveness. Right Action is more than just reaction. It springs from an attunement to the moment that the confines of convention obscure.

Tori's willingness to speak with the vice chancellor was like the monk carrying the woman across the stream. It was against her vows but she did it anyway. Rather than holding fast to her resentment, she stretched herself as the moment demanded. She took a step back and the unnecessary burden of being an aggrieved spouse dropped away. Something in her exhaled. Her mind, which had been carrying this anxiety for such a long time, was at least momentarily pacified. Her relationship with her husband, which had apparently come to an end, was suddenly alive again. Right Action, in this situation, meant restraining her initial impulses and engaging with the vice chancellor. While I would not define her intimate conversation with him as a flirtation, she was definitely flirting with disaster in talking with him. Her own internal proscriptions were strongly against it and her loyalty to her husband might well have prevented it. But she did not let her hesitation prevail. Having taken her daughter's advice, she had a surprisingly open conversation with someone she did not know as well as she thought she did. The forest inched a little closer to the castle walls.

Five

RIGHT LIVELIHOOD

Right Livelihood is the third of the ethical trilogy that began with Right Speech and Right Action. Classically, it means avoiding some of the worst qualities human beings are capable of: those involving deceit or exploitation. Examples from the Buddha's time include trading in weapons, buying and selling human beings, killing animals, selling drugs or other intoxicants, and manufacturing or distributing poisons. As these ancient examples suggest, things have not changed very much. People still make great fortunes in the very industries the Buddha warned against, although there are a few modern variations, like the trade in subprime mortgages, he could never have envisaged. Right Livelihood, from its inception, has asked people to consider the ethics of how they make their money. As with Right Action, the original idea was to protect the Buddhist community from its own most corrupting impulses with an explicitly stated set of moral principles. As satisfying as it might be to make money at other people's expense, the Buddha was sensitive to the covert cost to the mind. By introducing a clear set of moral precepts into the Eightfold Path, he was safeguarding his community from within and from without. His movement arose at a time of great mercantile expansion in South Asia when there was much money to be made. Right Livelihood suggested that this was a subject worth paying attention to.

In encouraging reflection on one's vocation, Right Livelihood brings up a number of provocative questions. What place does work have in my life? What is driving me? Do I have ethical qualms about my job? Does my livelihood define me? Is my salary the most accurate reflection of my worth? The Buddha said that most people are motivated by what he called eight worldly concerns. Gain and loss, pleasure and pain, praise and blame, and fame and disgrace are the ones he specified. He was careful not to judge people for these preoccupations, although he cautioned that they all come and go. Despite their relative impermanence, many of them are referred to with the utmost respect in the Buddha's ancient discourses. At one point the Buddha remarks that there are four kinds of happiness a householder should seek—"ownership, wealth, debtlessness and blamelessness"—and at another time he says there are five things which are "very desirable but hard to obtain: long life, beauty, happiness, glory and a good condition of rebirths." The Buddha was realistic about human nature and he understood that most of us subscribe, consciously or unconsciously, to a set of default explanations for why we do what we do. The most prominent of these, when it comes to one's livelihood, is money.

Money is not something that people talk about easily in therapy and it is not a subject I ordinarily offer advice about. People are much more comfortable, in these post-Victorian times, talking about sex than about money. They guard the details of their finances more religiously than their erotic fantasies. In my training as a psychiatrist, I was taught to bring up any business matters involving a patient—an overdue bill, a change in the fee, a payment that did not go through—at the beginning of a session. Getting it taken care of and out of the way allows for a smoother discourse thereafter. Allowing money to infiltrate a treatment by letting issues around it fester is a sure way to sabotage someone's therapy. But even if it is not an issue in the office, money is still a major subject in most people's minds. It is one of the primary means we have of measuring our self-worth. As an object of self-preoccupation and as a way of comparing one's self with others, it is right up there with how much we weigh. Right Livelihood encourages us to make this a legitimate subject of meditative inquiry, not just an object of private rumination. Money is a tricky thing for most of us. Many people make its acquisition the central focus of their lives, but some people, with a tendency to undervalue themselves, have trouble acknowledging how important it actually is. Both kinds of issues arise in therapy.

Right Livelihood asks us to pay attention to the eight worldly concerns and to try to find a place of balance within them. Do we chase praise, profit, pleasure, and fame as if they were the most important things in the world—as if once we corral them, they will last forever? Do we make our failures the linchpins of our low self-esteem? Do we judge ourselves on whether we can avoid pain and loss? If we allow our identities to rest only on such things, we

are destined for disappointment. There is always someone wealth-
ier, more famous, more recognized, or more accomplished than we
are, always someone with more likes on social media. The effort to
maintain one's status, wealth, youth, position, beauty, recognition,
or prestige can be an endless source of consternation. And the
self-criticism that surfaces under the spell of inevitable loss, pain,
blame, and disgrace can bedevil us for a lifetime.

The Buddha made Right Livelihood the centerpiece of the
Eightfold Path. Even those who renounced their occupations and
joined the Buddhist order were not spared its concerns. As part of
their vows, for example, Buddha's ordained followers were asked
to go out every morning to beg for their food from the nearby
towns and villages. This was an important part of their day, an
essential element of their livelihood. Because of their dependence
on the local communities for their daily nourishment, they were
actually related to as mendicants, or beggars, rather than as monks
or nuns. This connection to the outside world was important to the
Buddha. He did not want his *bhikkhus*, as they were known, to lose
touch with where they had come from or to think that a life devoted to inner reflection gave them a free pass from the concerns
of the outer world. The mendicants were a civilizing force in their
society, a reminder of the spiritual heights a human being could
achieve if freed from the need to support a family. They represented an ethical as well as a spiritual ideal. But the community
was a civilizing force for the mendicants as well. They had to explain their philosophy and lifestyle to the townspeople as they
wandered among them. They had to have something to offer in
return for their daily alms, and so they became teachers of the
Buddha's psychology, adapting themselves to the needs of those

who were feeding them. Their sustenance depended on their ability to maintain a fruitful relationship with the local people. They were some of the world's first psychotherapists.

Right Livelihood, in my view, takes inspiration from this. It asks us to pay attention to the quality of our interactions, not just to how successful the world tells us we are. "Right Livelihood is not only about what we do but also about how we do it," writes Joseph Goldstein. Because it is about our behavior in the world, it can also be thought of as Right Living or Right Relationship. Many people overlook this aspect of things. They see making a living as their essential task and are bothered when the competing demands of daily life intrude. They consider anything that detracts from their primary mission as a nuisance, as beneath them, outside the realm of the meaningful, and a drag. Right Livelihood suggests that money is not the only currency worth paying attention to. It suggests that many of us are locked into a formulaic way of thinking about work that gives too little consideration to how we actually behave. The ethical dimension of Right Livelihood does not have to be limited to a prohibition in trading weapons, drugs, or human beings. Right Livelihood encourages us to be ethically aware of how we interact and how we relate—not just to our level of achievement.

Many people find this essential teaching of the Buddha hard to swallow. If they seek meditation, it is with a not so secret hope of gaining a competitive edge in their work. They are not eager to look at the quality of their interactions or the hidden selfishness of their inner motivations. I am encouraged when meditation helps a person become more efficient, more relaxed, more attuned, or more creative, but I know these are temporary accomplishments,

as likely to be co-opted by the ego as not. Right Livelihood asks us
not to be satisfied with the superficial attainments of meditation.
The admonishments of the Dalai Lama to "get a life" and of Munindra to "live the life fully" speak directly to this. Right Livelihood
asks us to bring meditative understanding *into* the world just as
the original Buddhist monks and nuns did in their alms rounds. It
questions whether money need be the gold standard of our worth,
whether livelihood is only about the accumulation of wealth and
prestige. There is a lot of work to be done that does not fit into this
model.

I thought about this recently when working with an accomplished
installation artist named Gloria whose work is in the collections
of the Whitney Museum and the Museum of Modern Art in New
York. Gloria is at the top of her field and often installs her com-
missions in museums or in privately held collections. She has been
chosen for residencies at some of the most renowned artists' colo-
nies in the world and has been the recipient of several important
foundation awards. But even at this level of achievement, it is difficult for Gloria to feel she has arrived. Male artists are consistently more highly regarded—and rewarded—than she is, and no
matter how much money her work is sold for, she has to pay her
assistants, her studio rent, and her fabrication costs, while split-
ting whatever revenue she makes with her gallery. In order to sup-
plement her income, Gloria sometimes travels to individual
collectors' homes to install her pieces in their houses. While this
seems to me to be nothing to complain about, for Gloria it has become something of a trial and tribulation.

When Gloria first began doing these kinds of private installations, she was excited. She traveled to places like Aspen, Santa Fe,
Sun Valley, Palm Beach, and Jackson Hole to find spots within her
collectors' houses to place her installations. She had to do much of
the work on-site—it would take her close to a week to get everything right. After a number of years, these visits have begun to
make her weary. She does not like having to make conversation
with the wealthy collectors (who are unfailingly friendly and supportive of her) and she does not like being away from her partner,
her dog, her garden, her home, and her studio. The repetitive
nature of these situations has begun to get to her and she feels
constrained by the life she has created to support her creative
practice. She needs these jobs, but she resents them. She depends
on these collectors, but she does not want to be close to them. She
often thinks that male artists at her level of achievement have it
easier. They are paid more, are treated better, and would not be
expected to hold the collectors' hands in the same way. One of the
things she likes most about being an artist is working alone in her
studio. Now she has to spend weeks in other people's homes in-
stalling pieces she has already thought about. The joy of creating
new work has become submerged in the professional life of a successful artist.

In one of my latest conversations with Gloria, she was on Bainbridge Island in Washington State in the home of a collector who
had made his fortune as an early investor in Microsoft. I agreed to
have a series of phone conversations with her while she was away.
I know Gloria pretty well and have helped her find her balance in
these situations before. I was sympathetic to her plight; she is a
serious artist and the work of the installation, while challenging in

some intriguing ways, was not of deep interest to her. And despite the kindness and generosity of her hosts, Gloria felt burdened by the attention they demanded from her.

As we were talking, I started to think of my physician father. He had been among the first Jews admitted to his medical school and kept a box that we uncovered after he died filled with medals and awards dating back to his years in high school. But as ambitious as he certainly was, he rarely let it interfere with his concern for his patients.

When he was a visiting professor at a now shuttered Harlem hospital in the 1960s, for example, he startled the mostly white staff of this teaching hospital by sitting on the beds of the sickest and most indigent patients while making his morning rounds. He touched them, examined them, cared for them, took their histories, and treated them with respect. I heard from a colleague that this single visit had changed the culture of the hospital in subsequent years. The physicians, who had been keeping their patients at a distance and had no personal financial interest in their care, could see what those patients had been missing. And they realized that they were missing it too.

I told Gloria these associations when I was on the phone with her. She understood what I was getting at.

"The poorest of the poor," she exclaimed. "I have to have a care for it!"

Gloria had been disparaging the situation she was in, seeing it as beneath her while criticizing herself for being "dirty" for taking the money it provided. She saw herself in competition with her male peers and was resentful of the extra effort she was required to make and the lesser compensation she was afforded. Her aversion, her envy, her judgments, and her resulting self-loathing were preventing her from giving herself to her work in a complete way. She reminded me of my own hasty escape from my teaching day at the Open Center all those years before. My inclination then had been to remain in the safety of my own little world rather than make myself available to the task at hand. Right Livelihood was asking Gloria to be aware of her own entitlement so that she could respond in a less programmed way. She was correct in her perception of the way the art world favored men, but this did not necessarily justify her attitude toward her collectors. Could she confront her prejudices the way my father had covertly encouraged the local doctors to examine theirs? Could she get past herself and have a care?

Gloria had a real change of heart after our discussion.

"I, too, am the poorest of the poor," she exclaimed. Gloria was not equating the sexism of the art world with the racism of New York in the 1960s, although she could have. She was not seeing herself as a neglected patient in the hospital. She was recognizing the inner scarcity that came from her own withholding. Like the physicians in the Harlem hospital all those years ago, Gloria was depriving herself of the joy of giving. In her sudden acknowledgment that she, too, was the poorest of the poor, she realized this. Immersed in the wealth she was seeking, her inner life was poverty stricken. This was a real turning point for Gloria. Instead of holding herself aloof and resenting her predicament, she felt a stirring of humility. As the poorest of the poor, she deserved the same kind of compassion she was denying her collectors.

"You gave me a big burst of energy," she told me in a follow-up phone call. "I ate a simple dinner, sat and talked with my collector and her husband, and went to bed early. It was okay for once."

In giving attention to her patrons, Gloria was able to put herself—and her preoccupation with her livelihood—aside for a bit. This made everything easier and let her work proceed more effortlessly. She stopped comparing herself to other, more successful artists and was surprised to find that she was not feeling as sorry for herself. Her livelihood, rather than assuming the role of torturer, came more into perspective. Her ambition did not diminish, I hasten to point out, but her resentments did. Gloria saw that there was some reason, some purpose, in surrendering to the unwelcome aspects of her profession. There was something she could learn from stretching herself interpersonally as well as artistically. A previously untapped well of generosity began to emerge as a result.

This set of conversations with Gloria reminded me of a famous story from the Buddha's time. While it is not a story about an artist, or about a woman, it is very much about the potential of Right Livelihood to set a person straight. The story is as follows. Once, during his years of teaching, when the Buddha was camping in the countryside, his associates warned him in no uncertain terms not to go out walking by himself. A famous bandit, a murderer named Angulimala, had been sighted in the neighborhood. He was a fearsome fellow and Buddha's followers were right to be afraid. Angulimala had made a profession out of banditry. He had vowed to collect a thousand severed fingers and was rumored to have already garnered nine hundred ninety-nine. Against all advice, the Buddha set out for his walk. On seeing the Buddha from afar, Angulimala armed himself and began to chase after him. But no matter how fast he approached, the Buddha stayed the same distance away. Some kind of magic kept them apart. This went on until Angulimala became fatigued and fed up. Nothing like this had ever happened to him before.

Exasperated, he stopped and shouted out to the Buddha, "Stop, recluse! Stop."

Continuing on his way, the Buddha responded, "I have stopped, Angulimala; you stop too."

The paradoxical nature of the Buddha's response completely unnerved the famous bandit.

"While you are walking, you tell me you have stopped, but now, when I have stopped, you say I have not stopped. I ask you now about the meaning: How is it that you have stopped and I have not?"

The Buddha needed to employ his supernormal powers to get Angulimala to rethink his chosen livelihood. But once he had his attention, he held himself up as an example. He explained how he had stopped clinging to his exaggerated sense of self-importance, was no longer preoccupied with the eight worldly concerns, and had extinguished the fires of ignorance, greed, and rage. No longer driven by his ego, he did not have to attack or defend; he could just be. The Buddha spoke so convincingly that the murderer, who had never imagined another profession, did stop. He took on the robe and begging bowl of the Buddhist order and, despite the criticism of some of the faithful, became a trusted member of the Buddha's entourage.

The story of Angulimala is one I often think about when issues of work and family collide. Just as Gloria's expectations for her career kept her in a state of isolation and agitation, so do many people's notions of the centrality of their work keep them cut off from the people they need the most. When Gloria stopped her resentment at her patrons, she became a better ambassador for her art. In getting over herself, she moved from a familiar feeling of entitlement to an unfamiliar one of compassion. Unlike Angulimala, she did not need to renounce her chosen profession and put on monk's robes, but she nevertheless made an important shift in the way she was living her life.

Another patient of mine, a woman named Kate, made a similar shift. She, too, found that the confluence of Buddhism and therapy helped her get over herself. I think about Kate in the context of Right Livelihood because her issues also centered on a feeling of privilege associated with her work. Her difficulties did not arise at her job, however; they came when she got home.

Kate works forty-five hours a week in a clerical position at a midtown architectural firm. Her boyfriend, with whom she lives in a one-bedroom Fort Greene apartment, is retired. He does many of the household chores while she is at work: the laundry, the shopping, and almost all of the cooking. He usually has a big dinner waiting—more than she really needs, she says—when she comes home. But Kate's boyfriend's standards of cleanliness do not match her own. The other day she came home exhausted from work and found the apartment in disarray. The glass coffee table was littered with newspapers and empty coffee cups, the bed was unmade, clothes were strewn across the bedroom floor, and when she went to the bathroom she found the top of the toothpaste lying on the counter with the half-empty tube lying nearby. That was the final straw! She got angry and said something mean to him, something about the toothpaste and how much did he really care? How many times did she have to ask him to do the simplest thing? It would take about twenty seconds to make it right. Was that too much to expect?

Kate had lived with her boyfriend for more than ten years. They had been through a lot together and, despite the tensions in their relationship, had continued to find solace and sustenance with each other. I knew, when Kate began to tell me her story, where it was going to lead. Kate's boyfriend had a temper, too. He did not take her irritation lightly. He blew up at her and she ended the evening in the bathroom trying to calm down by smoking a cigarette, something they had both agreed she would not do in the house. They managed to stop the fight from escalating further, but did not speak for the rest of the evening. They had been civil the next morning until Kate left for her appointment with me. The tension she was carrying was still obvious, though, and Kate was full of indignation as she told me what had happened.

I had been through far more serious confrontations than this with Kate in the process of her relationship and I am sure she was expecting sympathy from me. But sympathy was not what I offered. I thought that Kate's attachment to being the breadwinner was making her unnecessarily critical of her boyfriend. He was trying to do his share, after all, at least in some important respects. He cooked, he shopped, and he was obviously looking forward to her coming home. Yet Kate felt that her boyfriend was not giving her enough support—she had to work hard at her job, put money away for retirement, and she deserved to come home to an apartment that was not a mess.

"Why not just do it yourself?" I asked. "If it's only going to take twenty seconds, why not straighten up when you first come home and then pour yourself a glass of wine or something? I know it's not fair, but it would be a lot less painful than this."

Kate did not immediately agree with me—I'm not even sure that after close to an hour of talking about it that she agreed with me—but she did hear me out. Her boyfriend had his strengths and his weaknesses. He was not exactly shirking domestic chores even if he was unlikely to straighten up before she got home. She could pursue her notion of what was fair or what was right or what she was due and try to get him to see her point of view, or she could stop. She could even do the unacceptable thing of taking on the tasks herself.

"I'm not your maid," she had yelled at him before taking refuge in the bathroom, and I knew that she would hear my advice as at odds with her promise to herself not to become just that. Because she was a woman, was she expected to do the picking up?

"You're not my mother," he had screamed back at her. This was doing nothing for their relationship, I thought to myself.

In giving Kate my advice, I thought about my own home. My wife might not agree with me, since she does not experience me as someone for whom a clean house is much of a priority, but I actually like it when the house is clean when I come home from work. On days when I arrive and no one else is there, I will usually put things in order before doing anything else. I'll distribute the mail, clean off the dining room table, put away my old newspapers, fold up the blankets on the couch, put the dirty dishes in the dishwasher, cleanse the refrigerator of its spoiling food, and run a sponge over the countertops. If my wife is home, I am much more liable to do nothing, figuring, much as Kate seemed to, that it is not my responsibility if someone is already there. Why is it easier for me to do these simple household tasks without resentment when I am alone? I asked myself. What meaning, if any, do I put on it if my wife does, or doesn't, clean up? I thought about it and then told Kate what I was thinking. It helped her to hear about my domestic life. It helped move the conversation from the principle of the thing toward a more open discussion about what it all meant.

As nice as it would have been to come home to a clean apartment, Kate was giving meaning to the mess that was not necessarily there. We could summarize it as follows: If her boyfriend really cared about her, he would take the time to pick up before she got home. While I could see her point (and while it might even be valid), I did not agree. Kate was making her suffering more than it needed to be. It was bad enough to come home to a messy house; it was much worse to come home to a messy house inhabited by a boyfriend who did not care about her.

"Just pick up when you get home and then forget about it," I suggested.

Was I just reinforcing some kind of negative stereotype of a Buddhist as a masochist or a stoic or an enabler? Was I suggesting service or surrender out of my own fear of conflict or as a brake on Kate's healthy aggression? Did she not have a right to get her own needs met? I struggled, internally, with these kinds of questions even as I told Kate what I thought. But I felt strongly enough about it to tell her.

In my head was the Buddha's retort to the famous bandit, "I have stopped, Angulimala; you stop too." Kate's mind was making a very reasonable request. Her outrage was understandable and the demand on her boyfriend was not extreme. Couldn't he just pick things up before she got home from work? Was that really so much to ask? But her mind was giving the situation a specific meaning and this was keeping her in its thrall. Buddhism teaches us to look carefully at such situations. Are we like Angulimala, garlanding ourselves with the severed fingers of our victims, stringing a necklace out of our resentments? Or can we see past our own points of view? Pride, it is often said, is the last fetter to enlightenment. If one can believe the ancient Buddhist psychologists, many other difficult emotions—anger, jealousy, and envy among them—are easier to work with than pride. Even among very accomplished spiritual people, it has long been acknowledged, the tendency to compare self and other remains. If Buddhism can teach us anything useful, it is to loosen the attachments we have to our own indignation.

"How do you use meditation in your relationship?" I asked an old friend in Boston, a longtime Zen student named Richard Barsky, many years ago, before his untimely early death from myeloma, when he was one of the only married people I knew.

"By letting go even when you know you are right," he responded.

When my wife reads this over—someday—she will roll her eyes. Yet I have always remembered this little conversation. Letting go, even when you know you are right, is not a bad thing to keep in mind. Most of us do not recognize when our egos are driving our behavior. We feel justified in our opinions and in our expectations. Right Livelihood, while encouraging us to reflect upon how we make our money and how we structure our lives, can also help us question our inherent sense of privilege. Letting go even when you know you are right is a challenge as great as the one the

Buddha gave Angulimala. It helps bring the lessons of Right Livelihood home.

There is another famous scene in the life of the Buddha that
makes a similar point. In the hours preceding his final enlightenment, when he is doing battle with his ego, the Buddha's
tormentors shoot volleys of arrows at him. Some people interpret
this barrage as representing the internal enemies of anger, intol-
erance, and pride while others see it as symbolic of the rage of external foes. Whichever interpretation one prefers, the outcome is
the same. The arrows turn into bouquets of flowers as they rain
down upon him. They do not hurt the Buddha, whose mirrorlike
wisdom has outmaneuvered his ego. The power of his understanding turns the arrows into harmless objects of beauty. He
stops them much as he later stops Angulimala.

A friend of mine, the artist, writer, and curator Phong Bui,
who grew up in Vietnam and came to this country when he was a
young man, told me how when he was a boy his Buddhist grandmother used to take him to the seven-storied Thiên Mụ Pagoda in
Huế, the tallest religious structure in Vietnam, where there is a
giant painted mural of this episode of the Buddha's life.

"Why do the arrows not touch him?" his grandmother would
ask. "Why do they turn to bouquets of flowers?"

The usual answer has to do with the Buddha's conquering of
anger. Because he has stopped his own angry reactions, the arrows
cannot hurt him. Bui's grandmother had suffered tremendously at
the hands of her in-laws. She had not come from their social class
and they had been very derisive of her for much of her life. She

might have interpreted the painting solely on that level, for she had endured much cruelty and felt much justifiable rage. But she gave her grandson a different explanation.

"Why do the arrows not touch him?" she repeated. *"Because he is not there."*

Bui's grandmother understood, in a profound way, what the Buddha meant when he told Angulimala he had stopped. The Buddha, in getting over himself, did not vanish. In fact, his presence became even more powerful, his "being" a vehicle of transformation for those around him. In this way, he became a true expression of advice not given. The arrows shot at him turned to flowers not because of anything he said or did but because of the power of his presence. He had stopped his ego, and those around him could feel it. Even someone as intent on murder as Angulimala was touched and able to change his ways.

Therapists, at their best, can inspire something similar in their patients. The grudges and resentments that people carry with them often make sense when looked at from a narrow perspective, just as working primarily for money and not thinking about one's impact on others does. But a therapist can offer a wider view. Livelihood means more than just earning a living. It means recognizing that despite the fluctuations of gain and loss, pleasure and pain, praise and blame, and fame and disgrace—or, indeed, *because* of them—we are all the poorest of the poor. As Gloria realized, marooned as she was on Bainbridge Island, "The poorest of the poor. I have to have a care for it!"

Six

RIGHT EFFORT

The classic depiction of Right Effort used music to illustrate how the ego's ambition can sabotage its goal. An energetic disciple named Sona came to the Buddha for help and advice. Meditation was frustrating him. Despite exerting himself to an extreme, Sona was unable to find the freedom that the Buddha extolled. Sona was a musician by training, a lute player, and the Buddha used this fact to give him specific instruction.

"Tell me, Sona," said the Buddha, "in earlier days were you not skilled in playing string music on a lute?"

"Yes, Lord."

"And tell me, Sona, when the strings of your lute were too taut, was then your lute tuneful and easily playable?"

"Certainly not, O Lord."

"But when, Sona, the strings of your lute were too loose, was then your lute tuneful and easily playable?"

"Certainly not, O Lord."

"But when, Sona, the strings of your lute were neither too taut nor too loose, but adjusted to an even pitch, did your lute then have a wonderful sound and was it easily playable?"

"Certainly, O Lord."

"Similarly, Sona, if energy is applied too strongly, it will lead to restlessness, and if energy is too lax it will lead to lassitude. Therefore, Sona, keep your energy in balance and balance the Spiritual Faculties and in this way focus your attention."

The Buddha was giving a lesson in meditation to the former musician, helping him relax his effort so that he could find ease in his practice. He was showing Sona that attention was his instrument now, that it could be tuned just as his lute had been, and that it was possible, and desirable, to keep it adjusted to an even pitch. As a musician, Sona was aware that this tuning was not a one-time thing. An instrument requires care. Keeping it in tune is an ongoing process, one that requires a steady deployment of energy to keep it right. Sona was encouraged by the Buddha's advice. He did not have to be at the mercy of his ambition. As he learned to observe his own mind, he found he could modulate his effort and adjust himself as circumstances required.

This is not always as easy as it sounds. Until one becomes familiar with one's instrument, it is impossible to settle into a good rhythm with it. Musicians are not the only ones to appreciate this. Athletes who have experienced being "in the zone" have an intuitive understanding of it as well. When they lock into their game, there is a sense of effort proceeding effortlessly. While they cannot make this effortlessness happen magically, some players develop a sense of how they tend to get in their own way. This awareness allows them to consciously adjust themselves. I have found that being a therapist is very similar. Many days a week, I see from eight to ten patients, an hour at a time, with only one break. Friends often assume that this must be exhausting, but on most days it is not. If I am doing my job well, there is no room for me to dwell on my usual worries and concerns. I listen in such a way that the time flows by and my energy is not depleted. My workday is a vacation from my ordinary self.

Beckett's psychoanalyst, W. R. Bion, used to say that a good therapist has to discipline the mind to be free from memory and desire in order to function optimally. I think he had it backward, in a way. When giving attention to a patient, I am automatically free from the weight of my memories and desires. I do not have to deliberately let go of them in advance; they simply disappear when my awareness is given over, in a sustained way, to another. My thinking does not stop, but I stop thinking about myself, unless it is somehow relevant to what my patient is telling me. Even trying to retain details of a session to put into a book feels like an unto-ward intrusion on the patient and on my state of mind.

Freud proposed that an analyst dwell in a state of evenly sus-pended attention and he emphasized that this was no ordinary state of mind. "The rule for the doctor may be expressed: 'He should withhold all conscious influences from his capacity to at-tend, and give himself over completely to his "unconscious mem-ory,"'" Freud wrote. "Or, to put it purely in terms of technique: 'He should simply listen, and not bother about whether he is keeping anything in mind.'" Although this posture of analytic attention is essential to a successful psychotherapy, with the exception of a precious few therapists like Winnicott and Bion, analysts down through the ages have found it enormously difficult to restrain their egos. There is a rich literature of therapists twisting Freud's words to allow them to bring back their usual mode of focal attention trying to zero in on the problem in order to offer an erudite interpretation. Buddhism showed me that evenly suspended attention is not an impossible ideal but a very real possibility. My instrument could be tuned as well as Sona the musician's.

My favorite part of the Buddha's discussion with the lute player is his recollection of the "wonderful sound" the instrument had when it was in tune. The Buddha was referencing the joyful aspect of things that comes out of Right Effort, something Sona might well have forgotten in his overly ambitious pursuit of liberation. The Buddha obviously wanted Sona to take pleasure in what the proper deployment of his attention could bring. Something similar can happen in therapy. There is a wonderful sound when a therapist is able to listen without judgments or preconceptions, when he stops looking for what he already knows, restrains his own need to prove how smart he is, and settles into a state of relaxed alertness. Patients are held in a special way by this mode of attention and they often come to unanticipated realizations as a result. "It must not be forgotten," wrote Freud in 1912, urging his followers to restrain their need to be clever, "that the things one hears are for the most part things whose meaning is only recognized later."

I saw this very clearly in my work with Debby, a woman several years my junior, who had been anorexic when she was in her late teens. When Debby left home and went to college, she took one look at the food they were serving in the dining hall and said to herself, "Well, I'm not eating this." And she didn't. It was actually the odor, not just the look of the food, that made her so repulsed. The smell in the college dining hall was similar to one she had hated in her fifth-grade cafeteria. Her family had moved in the middle of that school year and Debby had not found the transition easy. She never ate the meals served in her new school but at least she could bring her own lunch in those days. In college things were different. Anorexia took her over steadily and relentlessly and eventually she dwindled to something like eighty pounds.

There is an extraordinary strength in a person like Debby who regularly refuses food. The Buddha was aware of this when he gave his initial teachings on Right Effort because there was a rich tradition in ancient India of ascetics refusing all kinds of comfort and nourishment in the pursuit of spiritual growth. Right Effort, as a concept, was used to counter the influence of these ascetics and to find a middle ground between self-denial and the rampant materialism of the newly empowered merchant classes of his day. The Buddha described an optimal middle way between sensory indulgence and the rigors of self-abasement. Little did he know that several thousand years later, the founder of psycho-analysis would come up with a similar formulation in his descrip-tions of how to listen to his patients. Freud was not so concerned with finding a balance between sensory gratification and self-denial, but he was exquisitely attuned to how therapists could modulate their attention. They should not be too eager to step in and they should not be too remote and reserved. In describing evenly suspended attention, Freud came up with his own version of the Buddha's instructions. "To put it in a formula: he must turn his own unconscious like a receptive organ toward the transmitting unconscious of the patient." He used the newly invented telephone as a model. In his formulation, Freud anticipated Winnicott's notion of good enough parenting. Too much attention, in the form of indulgence, amplifies a child's anxieties, while too little attention, in the form of withdrawal, becomes neglect.

Debby knew nothing of the Buddha's teachings about Right Effort, or even of therapy, in her college years and proceeded, with very little outside help, to pursue her adult life while still in the grip of self-denial. After graduating from college, she moved to New York City, entered the workforce, and, uncharacteristically for someone with anorexia, gradually got better without significant therapeutic intervention. She was helped by her move to the city. In New York, Debby had a blank slate: she was free to configure herself outside of her familial relationships. A chance encounter with a friend led to a job in the fashion industry that put her in the middle of a community of young people. Her weight began to normalize as she felt more accepted by, and involved with, the people in her new life. She had a relationship or two and then got married and found that her eating issues, already on the wane, faded while she was raising her children. She loved being a mother and had good, strong relationships with each of her kids. Her own mother was still alive and living in another state, but her relationship with her had stalled at the time of her anorexia, if not before. Debby felt that their relationship, which she remembered as very close when she was a child, had never recovered. Her mother was ashamed of her, she thought, and had dealt with her illness mostly by ignoring it and hoping it would go away. That this strategy had worked was of little comfort to Debby. Her anorexia had receded, but so had her closeness with her mother. She missed her, even at this age, but rarely made the trip to visit her.

The issue with her mother had been brewing for a long time. I had a sense of it when Debby first came to see me several years before and urged her to visit as Mother's Day approached. But it was a tangled relationship. One morning, Debby relayed a complicated story about a conversation they had just had about her grown daughter's upcoming visit to her grandmother's house. The possibility of Debby joining her daughter had been raised, but it was not an easy discussion for Debby to have with her mother. Debby was, in essence, waiting for her mother to ask her to join them. She did not want to intrude on her daughter and did not want to make her mother uncomfortable. When her mother did, in fact, say something like, "Why don't you come, too?" it did not feel like a real invitation. It was too late, too off the cuff, and did not sound as if it really came from the heart.

"It feels like she doesn't love me," Debby said, and she was upset.

I had a little trouble, at first, taking her level of distress seriously. We knew that her relationship with her mother was strained. We had talked about it a lot. In relaying her current feelings, Debby was speaking as if she had never had this thought before. Why should it now be such a surprise that it feels as if her mother doesn't love her? Hadn't we gone over this already? I had to remember Right Effort in order not to get in the way of what Debby was trying to tell me. My initial reaction of "We know this already" was threatening to interrupt or derail her. Only when I restrained myself from reminding her of what we had already figured out could the therapy proceed. Once I kept myself quiet, Debby began to speak in a different way. Up to this point, we had talked a lot about her mother's aloofness. But now Debby was turning it around. She blamed herself for her mother's lack of attunement and responsiveness. She was fundamentally at fault. While she had difficulty saying exactly what it was about her that made her so unlovable, it was clear that this notion had been simmering for a long time.

It is always tempting in such situations to be reassuring and supportive. "Of course you are not unlovable!" I wanted to insist. "Let's keep the focus where it belongs. If your parents had not been so self-involved, we wouldn't even be having this conversation." Yet these kinds of comments would not have helped Debby much. She might have been grateful for my support but still stuck in an alienated and self-critical place, one that I would be subtly dismissing in my attempts to be positive. Debby needed to see how her own tendency to blame was holding her hostage. It did not really matter if she blamed her mother or herself—in searching for a concrete explanation for the flaw she felt in her relationship, she was actually hoping to magically repair it. If I aligned myself on either side of her argument, I would still be reinforcing an impossible wish. We could blame her or blame her mother or *not* blame her or *not* blame her mother, but we would still be heading in a backward direction trying to undo something that had already happened. I did not jump in with any such comment, however, committed to holding my tongue to see where things went.

My mind did go in an unexpected direction, however; I was not exactly silent inside my own head. Debby's therapy session came shortly after a provocative radio interview I had listened to by chance. I was driving in the car one morning, flipping impatiently through the stations programmed into the radio's memory, when I suddenly heard a familiar voice speaking in what seemed to be an unfamiliar context. It was a deep male voice that I soon recognized as Bruce Springsteen's. He was talking about how hard it is to raise children when one's own childhood was less than perfect.

"We take what is good from our parents and leave the rest. That's how we honor them," the voice was saying.

I was struck by the wisdom of Springsteen's comment.

There was a Buddhist flavor to it—a homespun way of talking that reminded me of Right Effort. In meditation, we are trained to not push away the unpleasant and not cling to the pleasant, but this was a little different. Not rejecting one's parents because they were imperfect, not trying to force them to acknowledge their shortcomings, not rejecting becoming a parent because of what was done to us, not dwelling on the scars one's parents created, not forcing oneself to pretend that one's parents were fine when they were not, but simply being able to take what was good while leaving behind what was not. Wasn't this awfully similar to letting go even when you knew you were right?

The source of forgiveness, Springsteen seemed to imply, lies in the realization that we are not solely products of what has been done to us, that there is something essential within us that is not necessarily tarnished by calamitous experience. While this contradicts many of the assumptions that a hundred years of psychotherapy has helped create in our culture, it is a notion that finds much support in the spiritual traditions of the East. In Buddhist cultures, there is a more willing acceptance of a capacity for generosity that is not dependent on external circumstances, not compromised by trauma or mistreatment, and capable of surviving destruction. While the classic Eastern route to accessing this inherent selflessness is meditation, Springsteen's comments suggest that the Buddha's choice of music to illustrate Right Effort may not have been accidental.

I did not relay any of this to Debby; I did not really need to. She did not experience my silence as indifference and she did not find my lack of supportive comments to be withholding. I think she felt my attention to be what it was: warm but not indulgent, receptive but a bit suspicious of her rush to criticize herself. She was giving inappropriate weight to a conclusion that, once brought into the light of day, revealed its immature roots. I could see Debby seeing this for herself, a certain equilibrium rising within her to meet it. Her tendency to blame herself did not disappear as a result, but she was able, in that session—perhaps for the first time—to recognize its spurious nature. This was the beginning of a gradual undermining of her deeply seated conviction about her own unworthiness, an erosion that would slowly and repeatedly take place in her subsequent therapy. She began a series of visits to her mother's house that allowed them to move past the frozen feelings of forty years earlier into a territory neither of them had envisaged. Her

mother, now in her eighties, was more open than Debby remembered her. There was a lot to catch up on.

The working through of Debby's connection with her mother
allowed hidden aspects of her relationship with her grown children to emerge as well. Debby had found much joy in being a
mother but she was aware of secret fears that her children might
reject her the way she had rejected her own mother. She told me in
a subsequent session how uncomfortable she was driving home
one evening after having had an enjoyable dinner with her twenty-
eight-year-old son, the eldest of her four children. He was leaving
for a year in Europe in a week or two and she was overcome with a
bad feeling after parting with him.

"What kind of bad feeling?" I wanted to know.

There was a discomfort in Debby's face that suggested something deeper than a mother's natural worry for her grown child's
safety or her sadness at being separated from him. She had a difficult time describing her feeling, in fact. It was complicated for
her. She felt alone and sad—that much was clear—although she
was going home to her husband and had a good relationship with
her other children, all of whom she was in regular contact with.
But there was a level of distress coming through as she tried to
answer my question that put me on alert. It was as if she were having a premonition that something terrible was going to happen
when he went away.

Before talking too much more about the feeling, though, she
told me how the rest of the evening had progressed. Upon arriving
home, she had gone straight to the kitchen and eaten potato chips
and ice cream. It was not the first time she had mentioned compul-

sive eating to me, but this was not something she brought up regularly. She was a vegetarian who was generally very careful about what she ate. On this evening, though, she had thrown caution to the wind. The potato chips and ice cream had put her into a kind of a daze.

"I was numbing myself," she said.

This was an interesting comment. What was she numbing herself from? It was murky. She did not exactly know. I encouraged her to look more closely at what might have been going on rather than just castigating herself for her culinary indiscretions. She must have been anxious, she finally said. When she got home and started eating compulsively, she must have been having anxiety. We could start there.

I knew she was having anxiety, of course, but I might have been tempted to rush right by it or to label it for her, depriving her of the experience of naming it herself. I might have assumed that she knew she was having anxiety when, in fact, it was not at all clear to her what she was feeling. As therapists have found, the naming of the feeling is different from the feeling itself. Feelings can percolate under the surface and make us act in ways we do not completely understand. When the feelings are named, the compulsive actions are often not so necessary. Buddhism plays something of a double game with this fact. Sometimes, when people are lost in their stories or in their repetitive thoughts, they are encouraged to come out of their thinking minds, out of the story, and into their bodies and their feelings: to experience them more directly and to appreciate how their emotional bodies are in continuous flux. But other times, when people are subject to inchoate feelings that push them around, it is more important to know the emotions accurately. Naming the feeling helps make it intelligible. It robs the emotion of some of its power and gives a person some space from it. Rather than proceeding, without thinking, straight to the compulsive behavior, naming the feeling allows for a pause.

"Oh, this is anxiety. What can I do about it?"

In Debby's case, parting from her son had precipitated her anxiety, but there was something intolerable in the feeling. It was not a simple thing for her. Her lack of clarity about her anxiety indicated to me that she might be uncovering something from an earlier time. It was tempting to go back to her childhood and question, once again, how secure she might have felt with her parents, even at a young age. This was fertile ground for conjecture, and in many of our previous discussions we had certainly fleshed out Debby's early history. It had put her anorexia in context and made it more understandable, less something that had just descended out of the blue. But in the back of my mind during this discussion was Bruce Springsteen's advice about Right Effort. I wanted Debby to be able to take what was good from her parents and leave the rest so that her relationship with her own children could be less encumbered. I did not orient the conversation around the past but tried to keep Debby focused in the present.

As we talked, it became clear that Debby was adding a toxic overlay to the separation from her son. Not only did she fear that the farewell would be permanent, she blamed herself for causing it, just as she had previously blamed herself for her estrangement from her parents. She was at fault, she had caused the disruption, and there was something the matter with her. The ice cream and potato chips protected her by putting her into a daze, but at the same time they gave her another reason to feel bad about herself.

They made it very concrete. She felt nauseated and bloated and castigated herself for getting fat. And there was shame at her behavior. She was proving to herself what she had long feared: that there was something wrong with her that made her unlovable. We were at a familiar place. Here was another opportunity for Debby to see this particular pattern.

The inspiring thing about Debby was that she could see all this even while being held in its sway. I could talk to her from a psychological place and also from a Buddhist one. The parting from her son was hard enough, I told her. Why not try to experience it just as it was, without the toxic overlay she seemed to be creating? Did she have to project her badness onto every good-bye? Did she have to be lovable *all* of the time? Why not use mindfulness to help? Mindfulness was one of the Buddha's main meditative tools. It was designed to help people cultivate self-awareness so that they could stay more fully in the moment and not be at the mercy of their most destructive thoughts. It discouraged clinging to the pleasant or pushing away the unpleasant. It could help with this kind of thing.

Here is one interesting thing about mindfulness, though. In the original Buddhist texts in which it was presented, it was often described as "mindfulness and clear comprehension," not simply as "mindfulness." The balance between immediate apprehension and conceptual understanding, between knowing the feeling and naming the feeling, was there from the beginning. In asking Debby to use mindfulness to examine her troubling emotional experience, I was also asking her to investigate it thoroughly, without jumping to conclusions. I thought of a case study I had long admired in which Winnicott made a similar point. While his imagery might seem shocking at first, his thesis was that therapists often sabotage their treatments by trying too hard to be helpful.

"The basis of the treatment at the present time is my silence," Winnicott wrote in his 1963 report. "Last week I was absolutely silent the whole week except for a remark at the very beginning. This feels to the patient like something she has achieved, getting me to be silent. There are many languages for describing this and one of them is that an interpretation is a male bursting across the field, the field being the breast with the infant unable to cope with the idea of a penis. The breast here is a field rather than an object for sucking or eating, and in the patient's associations it would be represented by a cushion rather than a source of food or of instinct gratification."

I love that Winnicott turned his silence into a field, a breast, and a cushion. He was not thinking about mindfulness or about Buddhism, but he still ended up imagining his patient upon a pillow, just as she might have been if she were practicing meditation. The pillow was his present-moment attention holding her while she explored what she was feeling. His psychosexual associations came from earlier work with mothers and their infants. One mother would offer her breast and allow her baby to find it for herself. She held the space open (like a field) and let the infant have the experience of discovery. Another mother forced her nipple into the infant's mouth. That baby had a completely different experience, more like that of a phallus (in Winnicott's vernacular) than a breast. In Winnicott's way of thinking, the first mother, who offers her breast, *is*, while the second mother, who forces the feeding, *does*. In my work with Debby, while not being as resolutely silent as Winnicott, my attention was functioning as a breast that *is*. It was a field and a cushion and it made room for her to unwind. This allowed her to be skeptical of her old ways of seeing things. Her issues did not turn out to be only about separation.

One of the things Debby discovered in paying attention to the comings and goings of her adult children was that these partings were infinitely more complex than they had initially seemed. When she thought back to herself as a young child, things seemed relatively simple. The loss of closeness with her mother had made her anxious. Fifth grade was a problem. From early adolescence, her anxiety made her worry that something was wrong with her, a notion she acted out on her own body. And now that she had children of her own, she could see that she was projecting that conclusion onto them. But as we worked with her childhood fears and anxieties, she had to acknowledge that being a parent filled her with other feelings as well. In a certain way, her childhood memories had been obscuring the intensity of her coexisting adult emotions. Many routine meetings with her children left her with an undercurrent of unnervingly poignant feelings. She had tended to overlook them, or to interpret them as nothing but reflections of her childhood estrangement, but we found that this did not do them justice. Alongside Debby's anxiety was the intense, if excruciating, love that a mother has for her children.

In Buddhism, there are said to be four "divine" states of mind: kindness, compassion, sympathetic joy, and equanimity. The "divine" properties are present to various degrees in all people, but they emerge in accentuated form in meditation, almost as a by-product, as people learn to relate to their egos in a new way. It is here that we can apply the analogy to athletes finding "the flow" when they learn to get out of their own way. When self-centered preoccupations quiet down, these more "selfless" feelings come to the fore.

Ancient texts compare kindness, compassion, sympathetic joy, and equanimity to the feelings a mother has for four sons: "a child, an invalid, one in the flush of youth, and one busy with his own affairs." Kindness is what a mother naturally feels for her young child, compassion is what she feels when her child is ill, sympathetic joy arises when she sees him thriving in the glory of his youth, and equanimity is what she knows when her child is grown and taking care of him- or herself. The Buddhist texts are nothing if not sexist in the preeminence they give to the mother-son relationship. But the metaphors are still apt in the present day—no matter how parent-child gender relationships are now configured.

As we worked together, Debby began to notice variations of these empathic feelings every time she saw, and parted from, her grown children. Having acknowledged her anxiety and named her unworthiness, these other feelings became more visible. The intensity of these "divine" emotions made her uncomfortable, however. She was not practiced in tolerating such strong emotions. Her tendency was to shut them down, whatever they were, and this kept her, to return to the Buddha's metaphor, slightly out of tune. Right Effort for Debby, in the context of all this, meant making more room for her "divine" feelings while not judging herself so harshly for her anxiety. In a very important way, she was able to make the therapeutic attention I offered her an instrument of her own psyche. Without a formal knowledge of meditation, Debby nevertheless came to know one of its major fruits. By not letting her anxiety intimidate or define her, she gained access to the array of connected feelings—kindness, compassion, sympathetic joy, and equanimity—that had been, up to that point, confusing her.

Therapy is a compelling tool of Right Effort. A skilled therapist can tell when patients are acting out an emotion but not really feeling it, when they are pushing away a feeling rather than acknowledging it, or when they are numbing themselves to escape from something that feels overwhelming. Right Effort seeks to create a context in which learned habits of indulging or denying feelings can be divested. These habits are the equivalents of stringing the lute too tightly or too loosely. Too tight is like the rigidity of people chronically clamping down on their feelings. Too loose is like giving feelings free rein, assuming that because we feel them they are "true" and must be taken seriously. Right Effort is an attempt to find balance in the midst of all this. From a therapeutic point of view, it means trusting that an inherent wisdom can emerge when we avoid the two extremes. This wisdom, or clear comprehension, is the emotional equivalent of a therapist's evenly suspended attention. Buddha believed that this emotional equilibrium was possible for everyone. Feelings are confusing but they also make sense. A therapist's job is to help bring this equilibrium into awareness. There is a wonderful sound when it dawns.

Right Effort, while it often counsels restraint, has also encouraged me to be myself with my patients. There is ample room, I have found, within the posture of evenly suspended attention, to interact in a natural way without artificially hiding behind the role of the therapist. This does not mean that I speak everything that

comes into my head, but it does mean that I give myself the freedom to trust my intuition and take some risks in what I say. This is
clear in recent work with another patient, a talented and resource-
ful woman named Martha, whom I have seen intermittently since
before she and her husband had a son twenty-five years ago. I had
not seen Martha for quite some time when she called out of the
blue and asked if she could come for a session. I assumed we were
meeting for the therapy equivalent of a routine checkup, but things
did not go as I had expected. One thing I have learned in doing this
work: no matter how well you think you know someone, they can
always surprise you.

Martha had just become a grandmother. Her son's girlfriend
had gotten pregnant and the young couple had kept their child. I
figured this was the reason for her visit, but she was nothing but
smiles about the baby when I saw her. Something else must be
going on, I thought; Martha seemed a little too cheerful. Was
she compensating for something she was uncomfortable about,
maybe something in her marriage? I waited and then took a
chance. Silence was not my first choice on this occasion.

"Are you and Chad still having sex?" I asked her.

"Just the other day," she said with a smile, a hint of pride in her
voice. Her face fell for just a moment, though. "Chad was happy. I
was just as glad when we were finished."

I looked at her questioningly. Martha was never shy about sex.
She was a dancer who had subsequently worked as a bartender, an
organic gardener, and a landscaper. She was comfortable with men
and with her body. She was flirtatious in an easygoing and street-
smart way. I always enjoyed it when she came to see me.

"I never really go to the doctor," she said.

I wasn't sure at first what she was talking about; her comment seemed a bit like a non sequitur. But after a moment I guessed what she might be implying.

"The gynecologist, you mean?" I asked her. "Do you have one you like?"

"I have a name on a piece of paper," she said. "I know where it is. . . . This is so embarrassing."

I was puzzled at Martha's sudden bashfulness. It was definitely out of character.

"Maybe some estrogen cream?" I wondered out loud. "You don't take any hormones, right?"

She nodded her assent and I said something more about how some women, postmenopause, find the cream to be useful if they are sexually active. Martha listened but at the same time seemed to be batting my comments away. Some kind of nervousness had entered the picture and I did not understand. It was time for me to wait. She changed the subject.

"I'm doing the eighth step," she said, referring to Alcoholics Anonymous. "You know the steps? I tried to make amends with my cousin and I couldn't. I don't know why. It was just a little thing. He had given me some papers to hand out when we were young and I threw them away but I lied and told him I had done what he asked. But when I tried to talk to him about it recently I couldn't."

I barely understood what she was talking about. Papers to hand out? Her cousin? What? I asked something about her cousin. He wasn't a big character in my mind; I hadn't really even remembered that she had a cousin who lived with her family. He was just a year older than she was, she reminded me.

"I told you about this once," she said. "When I was eleven, he started crawling into bed with me. A few years ago he brought it up. 'I'm sorry for petting you when we were young,' he said. I hate that way of talking. '*Petting* you.'"

Martha's face grew hard. I had only the faintest glimmer of her ever having mentioned this to me and asked her more.

"What do you remember?"

Martha remembered two incidents but thought that there might have been more. She remembered her cousin coming into her bed and she remembered waking up with him on top of her. And she remembered that her father, an alcohol-loving Irishman she adored and was very close to until these events, was never the same with her afterward.

"My cousin said my father caught him and put a stop to it," she said. "I was the best little girl before all of this. I wanted to be a nun. It was me and the nuns. In the next couple of years I was completely wild."

"How wild?" I wanted to know, and she told me how she once took three hits of mescaline without thinking and ended up in the middle of a highway flagging down a tractor-trailer that she got into and tried to steal. She did indeed sound pretty wild, even for 1968.

But the crux of Martha's story, despite the lurid details, lay in the way she had interpreted her father's withdrawal. In her mind, the shame she felt (and could barely acknowledge) around her cousin's molestation of her explained her father's rejection of her.

"In his mind I was some kind of whore," she said.

I wasn't so sure. Catholic fathers of his generation (indeed, *most* fathers of his generation) often moved away from their daughters when they became teenagers, finding it difficult to maintain closeness when their children started to become women. They were scared, I think, and retreated, leaving the girls under the auspices of the mother. I suggested to Martha that her father might have become more distant when she was a teenager anyway, that he was not necessarily blaming her for what had gone on between her and her cousin. He had stopped her cousin from molesting her, after all. He had at least done something to protect her once he knew what was happening. I was quite insistent in my comments.

"Dr. Mark!" she exclaimed with obvious relief. "This is why you get the big bucks."

Some lifting of Martha's shame took place in this session, some reequilibration of her self-esteem. Her lack of ease going to the gynecologist, her discomfort in the talk of sex, the ickiness she felt about her cousin's use of the word "petting," and the indignity she harbored about her sexuality all led up to the way she blamed herself for the loss of closeness with her father. Talking about it threw her into a state of uncertainty, and this uncertainty was good. Maybe she was not to blame. Maybe even the events with her cousin, as pivotal as they were in her psychosexual development, were not to blame. Maybe things were going in this direction anyway. There was no way Martha was going to stay aligned with the nuns once the 1960s and '70s hit, and little chance that the childhood connection with her father could weather her adolescence. That was not necessarily her fault, nor was it so clearly a direct casualty of her cousin's unwarranted advances.

But Martha's reticence at talking about her sexual abuse is characteristic of such things. I have seen people who speak of it only after years and years of coming to therapy. It took real effort for her to overcome her bashfulness and even broach the subject. I am sure she was not planning on talking about it, but something in the session allowed her to trust the impulse. Once the conversation began, many of her preconceptions came into view. Did Martha really have to blame herself for her cousin's advances? Did her father's emotional distance actually mean he thought she was a whore? Could she be like Springsteen and take what was good from her father and leave the rest and thereby honor her relationship with him rather than continuing to live in fear or self-reproach? In a certain way, Martha's self-concept was conditioned—and determined—by her cousin's unwanted sexual advances. Her self-image was stuck in that tumultuous adolescent time—it was masquerading *as* herself. Right Effort allowed me, in the midst of my doctorly banter, to listen to the spontaneous associations of her session and share my thoughts. Martha considered what I said to her and relaxed a contraction that had hardened over time, keeping her feeling bad about herself and cut off from the reality of her father's love. Martha's willingness to unburden herself, to examine and then let go of her long-held convictions, was what allowed her to move on. Her exuberant cry of "Dr. Mark!" indeed had a wonderful sound.

Right Effort is not only helpful in the psychotherapy office. It is relevant in any situation in which strong emotions or habits threaten to carry people away. It takes a different kind of effort to go to an AA meeting or call one's sponsor than it does to take a drink, for example. It takes a different energy to restrain oneself from saying something nasty than it does to lose one's temper. And it takes a more concerted strength to remain quiet around one's adolescent child than it does to give repeated advice when it is clearly not welcome. Right Effort suggests that it is possible, and often desirable, to gain control over one's ego's impulses. The precondition for this is the ability we all have, however underutilized, to observe our own minds.

A friend of mine, a sculptor I have known for many years named Sam, told me a personal story about his struggle to give therapeutic attention to his mind. We were at the opening of his new upstate studio. He had just finished building it on a vacant lot he had purchased after selling a building he had bought years ago when artists could buy cheap commercial real estate in Brooklyn. He had almost been unable to build his studio, however, because his next-door neighbor, a longtime resident of the community, had objected to the construction and brought the full force of the town's zoning board down on him. In a desperate, but very smart, move, Sam had hired an elderly local attorney to argue his case in court. Sam was a fighter by nature. He reminded me of my maternal grandfather and his brothers, amateur Cleveland boxers who smuggled liquor from Canada across frozen Lake Superior during Prohibition winters. He assumed that with the help of his attorney, he would vanquish his foe. Truth would prevail.

His lawyer, however, had a different strategy in mind. He was an intelligent man and he knew how things worked in his town.

"Sam," he said, "you are going to kiss ass."

When Sam told me this story, I laughed and laughed. Imagining him having to kiss ass was just so funny. It was the last thing in the world he would ever consider doing.

"Aren't I paying you?" Sam demanded of his lawyer, bristling at his advice. "Can't you be the one kissing ass?"

"No," the attorney said. "It has to be you. And when we are in court," he continued, "until it is time for you to speak, you are going to shut up."

Sam was unable to keep himself quiet during the proceedings, but every time he opened his mouth his wife dug her fingernails into his arm and his attorney reminded him very loudly to hold his tongue. He had meetings behind the scenes with his neighbor in which he was as deferential and respectful as he could be. The strategy worked. The neighbor was appeased and Sam got to build his studio.

"It was the hardest thing I've ever done," Sam told me.

Right Effort, in Sam's case, did not have anything to do with expressing his true feelings, however in the right Sam felt himself to be. Right Effort meant listening to his lawyer and restraining his need for victory. It meant being quiet even though he had something to say, letting go even though he knew he was right. Sam's attorney was as wise as any psychiatrist, Buddhist or otherwise, could hope to be. A peace treaty was better than a war.

Seven

RIGHT MINDFULNESS

M indfulness is the aspect of the Eightfold Path that has received the most attention in the West. It is the distinctive attentional strategy of Buddhism and has found acceptance in a variety of fields ranging from business to basketball to psychotherapy. Rather than restricting one's attention one-pointedly to a single object of awareness as in most other forms of meditation, mindfulness encourages a dispassionate knowing of thoughts, feelings, memories, emotions, and physical sensations as they come and go in the mind and body. The general idea is that it is possible to empower the observing self so that one does not have to be swayed by habits and impulses or taken over by one's inner critic. One learns to dwell in an enlivened awareness rather than being hijacked, sidetracked, or seduced by the usual array of thoughts and feelings.

What is not usually emphasized in the excitement over mindfulness in the West is that, from a Buddhist perspective, mindful-ness is an introductory technique. It is an entry-level practice whose purpose is to open doors to insight. Contrary to many peo-ple's preconceptions, being mindful is not the be-all and end-all of meditation. The Buddha, in a famous parable, compared it to a raft made of grass, sticks, and leaves that helps someone cross a great water. "What should be done with the raft once you have gotten across?" he asked rhetorically. "Should you carry it with you for the rest of your life or put it down by the side of the river-bank?" In making this comparison, he was trying to stop people from becoming overly attached to his method. While his warning was powerful, it has not prevented many over the years from fetishizing their technique.

The trick to Right Mindfulness is not to turn it into another method of self-improvement. As with Right Effort, it is possible to try too hard and override the subtlety and simplicity of what mindfulness is. In the traditional Buddhist texts, mindfulness is compared to a cowherd who, at first, has to be actively involved in corralling his flock in order to protect his newly planted crops from being devoured. After the crops have been harvested, how-ever, the cowherd can sit in the shade and rest, maybe watch with one eye open, barely doing a thing. His cows have only to stay within the perimeter of his awareness; there is no longer any dan-ger to the produce that has been brought indoors. If he is too en-amored of his role as cowherd, however, or if he has an immature view of what it involves, he might continue to poke and pester his animals, agitating them unnecessarily. Right Mindfulness is sim-ilar. At the beginning, one has to actively deal with the distracted mind, paying attention whenever it wanders in order not to be car-

ried away by its usual inclinations. After a time, however, mindfulness is just there. It becomes second nature. It sees the
distractions but does not get swept up in them. That is why the
comparison to the cowherd who rests under a tree is so apt. Mindfulness, once established, continues on its own steam. It hacks into
the mind to see what is there, and, out of this self-observation,
interesting, unexpected, and sometimes uncomfortable things can
emerge.

I have long been sensitive to how easy it is to become fixated
on mindfulness. The ego cannot help but try to co-opt the process.
Early Buddhist texts warn of this danger. Some amount of striving
is important at the beginning, but a shepherd who is too actively
trying to control his flock can sabotage the entire effort. "With
excessive thinking and pondering I might tire my body, and when
the body is tired, the mind becomes disturbed, and when the mind
is disturbed, it is far from concentration," reads an ancient discourse entitled "Two Kinds of Thought."

When I apprenticed with the Dalai Lama's Tibetan physician
while on a research grant in India during my final year of medical
school, I learned of a whole class of anxiety disorders unknown at
the time in the West. I had done a number of silent retreats by this
point and was well aware of how anxious some people become
when trying to quiet their minds. I was able to spend about six
weeks with the Dalai Lama's physician, and, knowing that I was
heading to a career in psychiatry, I was eager to find out whether
this kind of nervousness happened in Buddhist cultures as well as
in our own. It turns out that meditation-induced anxiety is very
familiar to Buddhist monks and was well cataloged in medieval
Tibetan medical texts. Meditators who try too hard to be mindful

make themselves agitated and depressed. Their minds rear up like
angry horses determined not to be brought under control by their
riders. Instead of lightness of being, forced meditation brings only
anxiety and a grim determination to proceed no matter what. Tibetan doctors have such afflicted patients do simple tasks like
sweeping the temple halls or chopping vegetables in the kitchen
rather than prescribing more meditation. They know that the
treatment for meditation-induced anxiety disorders is less meditation, not more.

The wisdom of the Tibetan physicians is important to keep in
mind as mindfulness takes root in the West. Much of our culture is
built on striving, and many people have trouble leaving this mind-
set behind. The very word "mindfulness" tends to encourage this
overly aggressive approach. It can sound admonishing at times,
carrying with it the injunction, "Be Mindful!" There is a ring of
the Protestant ethic to it. This is not accidental. First used in an
English translation of a Buddhist text in 1881 at the height of the
British colonization of South Asia, the term "mindfulness" came
into general acceptance in the Western world thereafter. But the
term is a Western invention. The original word in the language
of the Buddha's time was *sati*. *Sati* means remembering. Right
Mindfulness—or Right *Sati*—means remembering to keep an eye
on oneself. Its opposite is forgetting—or absentmindedness—the
kind of forgetting that happens all of the time when one is lost in
thought. The distinctive quality of mindfulness is that it remembers. Once established in the mind, it remembers itself. A clearer
description of what is meant by *sati* might be presence of mind.

I was reminded of this when lecturing in Oklahoma City about
the relevance of the Buddhist approach for the treatment of trauma.

There was surprising interest in the clinical applications of mind-fulness there. A big veterans' hospital with many patients with post-traumatic stress disorder was nearby and its staff was open to new approaches to its treatment. One of the counselors at my talk was a fifty-year-old man with a long white ponytail. He came up to me at a break; I had only a second to form an impression of him. A large, healthy-looking man, he was wearing a long-sleeved white shirt open at the collar. He was well put together, stood up straight, and had a very confident demeanor. I could see him driv-ing a pickup truck.

"You know," he confided, "I never use the word 'mindfulness' with a man in Oklahoma. People just don't like the sound of it."

"What do you say to them instead, then?" I inquired. I thought maybe he had figured out a whole new vocabulary.

"I just tell them, 'Go outside and close the door. Stand there and listen.' That's enough."

His comment went to the heart of Right Mindfulness. Rather than reducing it to another therapeutic modality handed out by the mental health authorities, his recommendation hinted at what is most compelling about it: the possibility of discovering some-thing unexpected by paying relaxed attention to one's everyday world. By letting his initial instructions be about dropping one's guard and opening one's senses, this therapist was heading off a very common misunderstanding. While it is true that we spend much of our time needlessly dwelling in thoughts of the past or the future, the ability to stay focused in the present does not, by itself, guarantee any kind of personal transformation. Being in the mo-ment is pleasant enough, but it is just a jumping-off place. I have encountered many people who, in making mindfulness their ulti-

mate goal, congratulate themselves on being able to keep their attention on their breath or in the soles of their feet for extended
periods of time, as if such abilities, by themselves, make them a
better person. A friend of mine confided that he tries to stay mindful when eating dinner with his wife, for example, but that this did
not seem to lessen the tension between them. I pointed out that he
would do better to engage her in conversation rather than hiding
behind mindfulness as if it were the newspaper. He saw my point,
but it had not occurred to him on his own.

Right Mindfulness opens up interesting opportunities for
honest self-reflection, but there is no built-in guarantee that these
openings will be used productively. The self does not give up its
grip easily—all of the same defense mechanisms that Freud out-
lined are still operative even when mindfulness is strong. It is possible to overvalue mindfulness, to remain attached to its form
rather than working directly with what it reveals. That is why the
intervention of the therapist in Oklahoma was so skillful. Rather
than dwelling on the method, he was trying to inculcate a state
of mind.

I have tried to remember this with my own patients. Instead of
teaching mindfulness to them directly, I have preferred to create
an interpersonal environment in which they can listen in a new
way, trusting that this mode of listening is what allows insights to
come. I want the visit to my office to be like going outside and
closing the door. I want it to offer a fresh perspective on things
without my having to give overly specific advice or guidance. Even
in therapy, people are stubbornly lost in their thoughts and im-
prisoned within the stories they repeat to themselves. They try to
use therapy the way many people try to use meditation: powering

through to get to an imagined place of cure. Right Mindfulness, like a successful psychotherapy, slows people down. It pokes holes in the facades we unwittingly hide behind. When we stand outside and listen, we have a chance to eavesdrop on the ego's endlessly obsessive self-preoccupation. With the senses aroused in a new way—if people are willing—they can step outside of themselves as well.

A chance encounter at a dinner party on the eve of Rosh Hashanah while I was writing this book drove this point home. Toward the end of the evening, I was talking with a retired attorney in his early sixties who had finished a successful career representing and running insurance companies. He was smart, engaging, and voluble. I liked him, but I did not think he would be particularly interested in my work. I told him a bit about the book I was writing, and about how for a long time I had been wary of giving overt Buddhist advice to my patients. When he heard about my Buddhist leanings, he surprised me by telling me how he had twice been to Massachusetts for intensive workshops in mindfulness-based stress reduction. These workshops, modeled after the retreats I was familiar with but stripped of their Buddhist language and theory, had helped him a lot, he said. He did not know much about Buddhism, but the practice of mindfulness, as he had been taught, had already been of great benefit to him.

I told him how impressed I was that he had given mindfulness a chance. To me, it was a sign of how it was infiltrating the popular consciousness and losing some of its esoteric aura. The fact that an Upper East Side attorney in the first flush of his retirement was seeking out mindfulness rather than golf said something of its new level of acceptance.

I actually knew a lot about the program he had been to. It was begun by an old friend of mine, Jon Kabat-Zinn, who had been a fellow student on the first meditation retreat I had ever been to back in 1974. I remembered his heavy black hiking boots gliding back and forth over an outdoor stretch of ground as we did our walking meditations together. Even then, Jon, who had a graduate degree in molecular biology from MIT, was conscious of how alienating Buddhist language or concepts might be for people in the West. In developing his program at the University of Massachusetts Medical Center not long after this retreat, he presented mindfulness as a strategy of stress reduction rather than as a branch of the Eightfold Path. Jon surprised everyone at the medical center. His patients responded to the treatment. Workshops like the one my new friend had attended sprouted up throughout the country.

"Let me tell you a story," the attorney interrupted. "Here's what happened to me there.

"In the midst of my second workshop in one of those nondescript hotels outside Boston, after a couple of days of mostly silent meditation, I was coming downstairs for a small-group discussion one morning, and as I was opening the door I heard a voice. No one from the outside world was talking to me, though; the voice was coming from inside my head.

"'It's time to forgive your mother,' the voice said.

"I have never heard voices," the lawyer assured me with a smile. "This was the only time anything like this has ever happened to me.

"My mother had been dead for fifteen years, but she was one of those super controlling, intrusive Germanic mothers who knew me better than I knew myself and used her knowledge to get inside and manipulate me. There was no escape from her when I was young and my self-confidence was terribly undermined. I did a lot of therapy in my thirties but I remained angry with her and mad at my father, whom I blamed for not standing up to her and protecting me. Even at my father's seventy-fifth birthday, when I gave a speech (which I am very good at) praising his accomplishments, I was conscious of how false I was being and it made me sad and uncomfortable.

"But when I heard the voice saying it was time to forgive her, I knew it was right. Mindfulness had shown me I could."

I was very moved by the lawyer's account. There was something incredibly affirming about it. An Upper East Side attorney learning a hospital-based mindfulness technique in a generic Massachusetts hotel conference center had a life-changing spiritual and psychological experience. He had heard a voice, but he was not insane. He had gone outside of his usual routines and stopped and listened and heard something unexpected. And he was able to let go of one of the long-standing pillars of his identity, his resentment at his domineering mother. His reporting was so sincere and refreshing, I could feel how light the forgiving of his mother had made him. Mindfulness, even when abstracted from its original Buddhist context, had surprised and opened him. Where had the voice come from? How could it be explained? What did attention to the moment have to do with forgiving his mother? There is mystery to Right Mindfulness even when it is experienced in a Marriott ballroom.

Often, as mindfulness has become a technique of stress management, it is presented in such a way as to emphasize its rational, objective, and scientific precision. While it certainly has this dimension, there is more to it than that. While mindfulness encourages a clear-eyed view of oneself and one's direct sensory experience, it also has a hidden agenda. Its mission is to put the ego into perspective so that empathy is no longer obstructed. The insights it encourages all head in this direction. In the ancient teachings, these insights are framed around basic principles like impermanence. How can we stay attached to things in the same way when we directly perceive that everything is constantly changing? Why cling to wealth, sex, pleasure, or opinions when one understands that nothing lasts? While it does not necessarily make the painful aspects of impermanence welcome—the Buddha did not call old age, sickness, separation, and death suffering for no reason—it does help people become more accepting of that which they cannot control. Mindfulness brings transience into the foreground; it makes it incontrovertible. It gives a ringside seat on something we all know to be true but do our best to ignore. There is no escaping impermanence when practicing mindfulness. Resistance, as they say, is futile.

In confronting people with the reality of impermanence, mindfulness also acts as an agent of change. This is where its hidden agenda becomes relevant. In rubbing up against the underlying fabric of impermanence, in seeing it in both the outside world and the inside of the mind, one thing becomes increasingly apparent. Muttering under our breath is a grown-up version of the child we used to be, and one of its main refrains seems to be something on the order of, "What about me?" This self-important—and vo-ciferously insecure—internal cry is a superficial manifestation of our most primal attempt to both control and avoid the way things are. As infants, we are lucky if there is one person in the world—our mother—who treats us as though we are the center of the uni-verse. But even if we are given this essential luxury, it cannot last. Disillusionment comes quickly. While one's internal protests and manipulations are generally not successful, they do not necessar-ily go away. As the self develops, the need to maximize the feeling of self-importance persists. There are competing demands, of course—we are social creatures and selfish motivations are not the only ones we are capable of—but even very well-adjusted people harbor a self-centeredness that becomes obvious once one pays attention to the mind. Right Mindfulness takes great delight in bringing this self-centeredness to the surface. Egotism starts to feel painful and one discovers that one can step away from it. In a world in which nothing is as fixed as it seems, it comes as a great relief to discover that even the ego is impermanent. One's defen-sive posture does not have to be etched in stone.

Forgiving of one's mother does not show up on the traditional list of liberating insights, but if the list were being compiled in this day and age it would be near the top. Classical descriptions of mindfulness are derived from a tradition thousands of years old, but there are no reliable first-person accounts of the inner life of a person in the Buddha's time to refer to. We are living in a different time and culture from the Buddha's. Personal psychology is a re-ality for us. Insights, when they come now, while rooted in the re-ality of impermanence, are often of a psychological and emotional nature. The unfolding of mindfulness, while often presented as an orderly process, is different for everyone. Those who are not attuned to this truth risk missing out. The psychological aspect of Right Mindfulness is essential to a real appreciation of it.

Developing mindfulness is like learning to ride a bicycle or walk a tightrope, only much more frustrating. One keeps falling, even after years and years of effort. Right Mindfulness means having a light touch. It means being able to forgive yourself, time after time, while at the same time not giving in to your worst impulses. I remember being in Colorado one summer with Jack Kornfield, who had already had years of intensive meditation experience. Jack came to dinner on his birthday after spending the day in meditation, cursing himself for not being able to follow his breath for any substantial time that day.

"Even on my birthday!" I remember him complaining ruefully.

There was a hint of self-mockery in his comments, but he was serious. I was touched by his honesty. It helped me with my own practice, with my own tendency to be unforgiving. It helped me understand that Right Mindfulness means being willing to bring the mind back whenever one notices that it has wandered. It is the ability to bring the mind back, to let go of one's personal commentary, that is the real accomplishment. Thinking selfishly is one of the things the mind does best; even when it becomes very still, this tendency is still latent. But the ego does not have to define us, any more than my friend's resentment at his mother needed to define him. One reason he was able to forgive her was because, in learning mindfulness, he had practiced forgiving himself over and over again.

I have experienced my own version of this throughout the course of my involvement with mindfulness. Since my early twenties I have been practicing in a series of silent retreats of several weeks' duration. These retreats limit the amount of outside stimulation and distraction and are structured so that it is possible to make every basic activity—from walking, eating, and sitting, to caring for one's bodily functions—an opportunity for mindful attention. As difficult as this can be for the first several days—the mind rebels and wants to go its own way—after a while the act of remembering becomes more natural. One's self-awareness grows, or expands, so that one feels in tune with one's surroundings, present and very alive. Awareness, which we generally take for granted and which is usually transparent or invisible, starts to become something intriguing in its own right. At times it seems to glow. While thoughts, memories, and associations still continue unabated, one is less likely to be swept away for long periods of time by them. It is much more intriguing, and pleasurable, to abide in the unfolding present than to slip back into habitual trains of thought.

These retreats have almost always been interesting, even though, when one tries to talk about them, they sound rather boring. From one perspective, almost nothing to speak of happens. The day comes and goes. Meals are served. The sounds of nature fill the meditation hall. People sit on their cushions, shift, cough and stretch, or walk slowly back and forth in a straight line, eyes downcast, going nowhere. No one makes eye contact or speaks. But from another perspective, there is a lot going on, much of it personal and psychological in content.

On my most recent retreat, for example, I had the vivid sensation, some days into it, of my name imprisoning me. It is difficult to describe the actual feeling because it took place in an instant and reverberated in several directions at once.

"Mark."

Its sound was so hard. In the relative quiet of the retreat, it felt like the blow from a hammer or like an industrial stamp coming down on me from above. I imagined my parents saying "Mark" when I was an infant and me rising to meet their voices, willingly but with a reluctant whiff, the name gathering around me, a little stiff, closing me in. It made me sad, that sense of being oppressed by my own name; I felt how unyielding its tireless walls had been.

Almost simultaneously, though, I felt the possibility, or the memory (I am not sure which), of my name having nothing to do with me. It was just a glimmer, a stirring, like hearing a breeze in the distance and wondering if I was imagining it. Mark was my name but I was not Mark—that seemed to be the point. All around me, stretching in every direction, humming ceaselessly, was something alive and open. With the subtlest of effort, I toggled back and forth between the two feelings: "Mark," the feeling I knew by heart but felt aversion to, and "not-Mark," a new (or was it old?) sensation I could not quite put my finger on. I had several epiphanies on this retreat, but this one lasted for a fairly long spell. I remember it was interrupted when I checked my cell phone to see if I had any messages.

I am in the habit of keeping my phone with me on retreat, al-

though it is frowned upon. If my children or my wife or my patients need to get ahold of me in an emergency, they can reach me
directly. I was also planning, since I was bringing my phone anyway, to ring my mother on Sunday at four thirty as I always do. She
finds Sundays particularly wearisome and looks forward to hearing from me. I had just called her on my drive there and told her I
was heading to the retreat.

"I don't understand why you do those things," she had said
with a hint of exasperation.

They have a soundproof room at the meditation center for calls
like this.

I planned to keep my phone in a drawer, but I ended up keeping it on my desk. I did not carry it with me. That is the main thing.
I did not even wear pants with a pocket most of the time. I am in
the habit of checking my phone when I go to the bathroom—I don't
know how common this is, but it is definitely something I have
noticed I do. On the retreat I would find myself, at least for the first
five or six days, reaching for it whenever I peed.

"Reaching, reaching," I would say to myself, trying to bring
mindfulness to every moment of the day, noting the little blip of
anticipatory excitement when the thought came of checking the
phone and then the calm of restraint when I realized it was not
there.

It was a relief to be unplugged from my phone, even this much,
although I did miss it, especially when I went to the bathroom.
They say there is a burst of serotonin in the brain when one gets
ready to check one's phone, the anticipation of a reward, like
M&M's in a classic behavioral experiment or the rice crackers and
peanut butter at teatime, making the neurons leak their precious

fluid. Based on my own experience on the retreat, I can believe it. The urge runs very deep.

I managed to keep my phone under reasonable control throughout the ten days. I checked it only three times a day, as often as I ate, and the calls I received were minimal. But I did allow myself one indulgence. Every afternoon after lunch I would curl up on my bed with my phone and check the weather. There were three major snowstorms during my time there and the temperatures were regularly below zero. I went out walking around a frozen lake every morning dressed in six layers of clothing, and tracking the weather seemed like a vital, if harmless, activity. It *was* harmless, I'm sure, but my enjoyment of it made me wonder if I was cheating.

But did I need to beat myself up over this? Could I back off the judgment a little? I was in a tussle with myself around such a superficial infraction, if it was even an infraction at all.

Shortly thereafter, I was doing walking meditation in the basement gymnasium beneath the meditation hall. I was alone in the gym, or at least I thought I was, and my mind was fairly still after days of practicing mindfulness. I often resist the walking meditation; it involves little more than pacing slowly back and forth in a straight line. "Lifting, moving, placing," one repeats to oneself as one directs the mind's attention to the bottom of the feet. I find it difficult to keep this up for more than fifteen minutes or so; my back often starts to hurt and I stop and stretch and look for excuses to do something else. On this occasion, however, I was less restless than usual and was aware of a certain ease creeping into the exercise. The walking felt a bit like swimming laps. It was smooth and rather effortless.

Then, out of nowhere, came a loud slap. I jumped, turned around, and saw that a wooden or bamboo Chinese screen had clattered to the ground behind me. The screen had been walling off a small area set aside for the practice of tai chi. I had never noticed it, nor had I ever entered the space behind it; the screen was simply, for me, part of the immovable furniture of the rather drab room. But now it was lying flat upon the ground; someone must have brushed past and knocked it over. The interesting moment came next. Because my mindfulness was strong, my immediate mental reaction was very apparent.

"Who did that?"

This was not an incidental and curious thought. It was a vengeful one, my mind immediately wanting to reproach someone. Right away, I needed someone to blame. The thought shot up like a rocket but stopped short. It actually froze in midair. I saw it visually. It was like a firework that took off very quickly but could find no traction. It did not take hold—it just died there in inner space. I do not usually see my thoughts as pictures, but in this case I did. I saw the spaciousness of my mind and the incidental nature of the thought. It was like seeing a match being struck but then fizzling out. I laughed to myself. It was absurd to be casting about for someone to blame. What did it matter? What was I trying to prove?

There was a severity in me, I realized, a severity I had not completely owned. It showed itself vividly when the screen toppled over, but it was there when I felt the oppression of my name and when I judged the checking of my cell phone. With respect to my name, I wanted to hold someone responsible in much the same way as when the screen fell. Who did this to me? I did not like it. It must be someone's fault.

This need to blame is of course a very common one. I come up against it all the time in my work as a therapist—in myself and in my patients—and I am often aware both of how alluring it can be and of how people are better off without it. But this moment on retreat had a special power. I actually saw the impulse to blame come into being and then saw it cease. Right Mindfulness allowed me to see it in the same way that it allowed my attorney friend to forgive his mother. In seeing how instinctive the need to blame was for me, I was chastened. But in seeing that it did not need to take hold, I was released. Events like the clattering of the fallen screen happen all the time in my life. Someone drops something, spills something, bumps into me. I wait on the phone to speak to a representative and then get cut off. My credit card bill is incorrect; someone has charged things on my account. My friend says to meet him at six thirty for dinner and shows up forty-five minutes late. Someone leaves garbage in front of my building and we get a ticket from the sanitation department. There is always something.

This single experience in the gymnasium beneath the meditation hall changed things for me. I relaxed about my cell phone. I stopped chafing at my name. I called my mother the following Sunday from the soundproof room. I still had three days left in my stay. We had a good conversation, for maybe ten minutes or so. She seemed to have forgotten that I was at the retreat; maybe I hadn't made it totally clear to her that I was going for ten whole days. As our talk was winding down, though, she suddenly asked me where I was.

"Are you in the country?" she said.

I often called her from our house in the Hudson Valley, so her question was not unusual.

But she quickly added, "I don't know why I'm asking; it doesn't really matter."

I prevaricated. I did not want to remind her that I was still at the retreat, and I quickly told myself that since the retreat was in the countryside, I could say yes without feeling too guilty.

"Yes," I said. "I'm in the country."

I felt bad for not telling my mother the whole truth, but I forgave myself quickly. I understood why I said what I said. While I was protecting myself from her judgment, I also did not want to make her worry. The important thing was that I'd called when I said I would. My inner critic did not have to use this against me. As I realized when the screen fell in the empty room, my need to find fault did not always have to have precedence.

Revelations on retreat come incidentally and poke holes indiscriminately. As in therapy, progress cannot always be predicted. My name, my speech, my phone, my bed, my moments of reaching in the bathroom for what was not there, my instant of clarity in the walking room. Each one of these situations let me see myself in more relief and brought the threads of my identity more into focus. The practice of Right Mindfulness helped direct my attention to these little bits of experience. I might well have overlooked them were it not for the Buddha's insistence that the mind was worth watching, even when doing nothing. There was an unexpected dividend to all of this heightened attention. Maybe, in the future, I would not have to let my severity drive me so much. Maybe I could stop looking for someone to blame, let my flaws settle and meld with the rest of me, stop taking my name—and my self—so seriously.

Right Mindfulness, and the self-scrutiny it engenders, builds a mental muscle. It is a muscle of nonjudgmental self-observation, but it can become much more than that. It is also a precursor of insight. The form such insight takes is different for everyone, but the flavor is similar. Mindfulness makes use of all of those throwaway thoughts that harken back to our childhoods, the ones we adopted to cope with the pressures of growing up. In asking us to pay attention to their repetitive nature, mindfulness also encourages us to recognize their childish quality. My moment in the walking room, in which I saw my need to blame, was another version of the voice in the lawyer's head that showed him how unforgiving he had been. In both cases, we were stopped in our tracks and made aware of how unnecessary such self-protective responses could be. Given the freedom to act differently, we both made a similar choice. Mindfulness showed us how.

Eight

RIGHT CONCENTRATION

C oncentration is the secret ingredient of meditation, the backbone of the entire endeavor. It is the simplest, most elementary, most concrete, most practical, and most ancient therapeutic technique in the Buddhist repertoire. It is a means of temporarily dispelling the repetitive thoughts of the everyday mind, a way of opening the psyche to new and unscripted experiences. Although it follows mindfulness on the Eightfold Path, it is generally taught *before* mindfulness when learning to meditate. It is such an essential introduction to Buddhist practice that its closing place on the Eightfold Path does not make sense at first glance. But concentration needs to be understood in the context of the entire path if it is not to become a distraction in itself. Concentration is "Right" when it connects with the other branches of the whole. It is "Right" when it demonstrates the feasibility of training the mind, when it supports the investigation of impermanence, when it erodes selfish preoccupation, and when it reveals the benefits of surrender. It is not "Right" when it is seen as an end in itself and when it is used to avoid painful truths. One can hide out in the peaceful states that meditative concentration makes possible, but in the context of the Eightfold Path, this is considered a mistake.

Concentration, from a Buddhist perspective, means keeping one's attention steady on a single object such as the breath or a sound for extended periods of time. This is not something that we do ordinarily and it is not something that comes easily. Those who try to fix their attention in this way for even five minutes will see this for themselves. Try to follow your breath and see what happens. Note the sensation of the in breath and repeat the word "in" to yourself. Do the same with the out breath and repeat the word "out." Keep the mental label in the background and the bulk of your awareness on the direct physical sensation of the breath. If you are like most people, after successfully noting a breath or two, your usual subconscious inner world will reassert itself. Thinking, planning, fantasizing, and worrying will rush to fill the void, noises from the outside world will pull you in, and five minutes will be over before you know it. The mind does not become concentrated just because we tell it to.

But Right Concentration asks us to persevere. Beginning meditators struggle with this very simple task. Whenever they notice that their attention has strayed, they return it to the central object. Lapses in attention happen not once or twice but over and over and over again. Sometimes people notice right away, and sometimes not for a long while, but Right Concentration suggests that we do not judge ourselves for our failings. Ancient texts compare the process of concentration to the taming of a wild animal. It is a difficult endeavor, full of ups and downs, but one that yields reliable results if practiced diligently and with patience.

As concentration increases, the mind and body relax. Thoughts diminish, emotional pressures weaken, and a kind of calm takes over. The mind gradually comes under some degree of control and settles down. The Buddha compared this process to the smelting of gold. When its superficial contaminants are removed, gold becomes light, soft, malleable, and bright. Its brilliance comes forth and it begins to shine. Western scientists who brought experienced meditators into the laboratory have documented a physiological version of this. When one-pointed attention is strong, the nervous system kicks into a relaxed mode. Heart rate slows, metabolic rate declines, digestion picks up, and brain activity associated with worry and agitation goes into neutral. It was a major surprise for Western scientists to find that something as simple as concentration could have such profound effects on the body. Few researchers thought the so-called involuntary nervous system could be brought under conscious control. Buddhism, for thousands of years, has made the case that concentration brings calm and tranquility to both mind and body. Western science has documented this in terms of the body's physiology, even if the mind's golden nature has proven more elusive to direct confirmation.

The benefits of concentration for the management of stressful situations are now widely acknowledged. I spoke recently with a young man newly diagnosed with colon cancer who had to go through a number of tests, scans, and procedures in rapid succession. His wife was interested in meditation and had already begun to explore it, but he had other things to do when he was healthy.

Upon receiving the diagnosis, however, he needed something to help him, and he quickly became proficient in using concentration to calm his anxiety. This was incredibly useful. When inside the PET scan machine, for example, where he had to lie still for long periods of time in a close space, he was able to watch his breath or scan the sensations in his body while letting the machine do its thing. It was just like a long, enforced meditation, he told me cheerfully, and it was fine. It is good to have this ability, to know from experience that it is possible; it is incredibly useful in all kinds of uncomfortable situations.

Concentration is not just a method of managing stress, however; it is also an incubator of self-esteem. This is less easily measured but just as important. I found this out for myself during one of my first extended explorations of meditation. Up until this first retreat, I had tried to watch my breath with varying degrees of success. I was taken with the challenge and interested in the underlying philosophy of Buddhism, but my immediate experience of meditation had mostly made me aware of the rather mundane nature of my own mind. The more I tried to watch my breath, the more I saw of the incessant, routine, repetitive, and self-serving thoughts running through the undercurrents of my psyche.

At this retreat, however, after about three or four days of practice, things started to shift. I remember sitting in the meditation hall and suddenly being able to focus. All the effort to locate the breath and stay steady with it no longer seemed necessary. It was just there. Although I was remarkably devoid of my usual litany of thoughts, I was wide awake and clearheaded. My eyes were closed in the darkened hall, but light started to pour into my consciousness. Literally. I was seeing light while resting the bulk of my attention in the breath. The light lifted me in some way and I had that feeling I sometimes get, when very moved, of the hairs of my body standing on end. A strong feeling of love came next—not love for anyone or anything in particular—just a strong sense of loving. This all lasted for a while. I could get up and walk around and then, when I sat back down, it would be there again. It was as if the curtains in my mind had parted and something more fundamental was shining through. It was tremendously reassuring. Many of my doubts about myself—as inadequate, unworthy, or insufficient— seemed, as a result, to be superfluous. I knew, from the inside, that they were stories I had been repeating to myself, but not necessarily the truth. The love pouring out of me seemed infinitely more real.

While this experience lasted for hours, it did not, of course, last forever. It was one of the more dramatic things to ever happen to me while meditating, and, in fact, I subsequently spent a fair amount of time trying to get it back. But its impact is as strong today as it was when it first happened. I know for a fact that behind my day-to-day preoccupations lies something more fundamental. While I have changed over the years, and while change (as we know from Right View) is the nature of things, this underlying, almost invisible, feeling is there in the background. Concentration revealed it to me and sometimes allows it to reemerge. At times, with my family, with my patients, when listening to music or walking in the countryside, it peeks through of its own accord.

A couple of years after this pivotal experience, when I was in medical school and doing one of my first monthlong rotations in psychiatry, I had an individual tutorial with an esteemed

Harvard psychiatrist, Dr. John Nemiah, who was teaching me about a rare syndrome then called "conversion hysteria." In this disorder, patients present with physical, often neurological, symptoms, like paralysis or shaking fits, for which no organic cause can be found. In many such cases, the theory goes, the actual problem is some kind of anxiety, but the anxiety is "converted" into physical symptoms because it is too overwhelming to experience in its raw psychological form. The diagnosis is rarely used today; it has been replaced in many instances by the term "dissociative disorder," and some clinicians now believe that the symptoms can be traced back to episodes of sexual abuse. But the underlying theory about it remains essentially unchanged. Overwhelming feelings are somehow displaced onto, or into, the body. Physical symptoms emerge that have no direct and obvious cause. Post-traumatic stress might be thought of as a contemporary version of this. Traumatic events, never fully acknowledged, come back to haunt people in the form of seemingly inexplicable symptoms that arise as if out of the blue. Dr. Nemiah showed me some films of patients from the 1950s with conversion symptoms and then questioned me about them. He was trying to teach me not just about this particular syndrome, but about the concept of the unconscious. If a patient's symptoms are expressions of underlying anxiety, he wanted to know, how do they get "converted" into physical form? How does this happen?

"What *is* the unconscious?" Dr. Nemiah asked me. This was a central question for a young would-be psychiatrist in those days, and I sensed that his evaluation of me depended upon my answer.

I thought immediately of my retreat, of the curtains parting and the light shining through, of my understanding that the narrow world of my day-to-day preoccupations did not have to define me. In Dr. Nemiah's world, the unconscious was mostly thought of as the dark and lurking place from which dreams emerge, but, as much as I would come to respect that point of view, this was not how I was thinking at the time.

"The unconscious is the repository of mystery," I responded.

I remember how much Dr. Nemiah liked my answer despite being unaware of what I was actually thinking about. I was not about to tip my hand to him about my Buddhist leanings despite my admiration for his clinical acumen. Buddhism, at that time in my life, was not something I was talking about to my superiors, especially those who were going to give me an evaluation. But my answer worked just as well in his world as it did in my own. Mystery encompasses the dark as well as the light.

As an experienced and erudite psychiatrist, Dr. Nemiah was trying to give me a feel for how little we, as supposed experts, understand the recesses of the mind. The unconscious *is* a mystery and it remains one all these years later. In bringing Buddhism to a Western audience, I am in a similar situation. As much as I might talk to my friends and patients about how concentration opens doors into unexpected areas of the psyche, nothing beats experiencing it for oneself. Concentration is a channel into something we do not have exact words for. The unconscious? Mystery? The imagination? Love and light? It is tempting to turn whatever it is into something more concrete than we can actually apprehend.

Right Concentration argues against doing this. I think that is why it is saved for the last step instead of being talked about at the beginning. Right Concentration does not want us to get attached to it. It does not want us to turn it into an object of worship. Use it to

free yourself, but don't turn it into another thing. Allow it to remain unpredictable.

My Buddhist teachers, in making this point, chuckle at a story
they often repeat. A man who successfully completed a three-
month silent retreat came running down the street in its immediate aftermath screaming, "It didn't work. It didn't work." Under
the spell of developed concentration and enveloped within the silence of the retreat, this man had discovered a profound sense of
inner peace. Mistakenly assuming that this achievement was permanent and that his mind had been transformed (and laboring
under the conviction that absorption was the goal he was aiming
for), he was naturally distressed to find this golden state evaporat-
ing as soon as conditions changed. He thought his mind would stay
quiet forever and assumed he was finally rid of his neurotic tendencies. But his assumptions were unfounded and his attachment
to a particular state of mind was revealed.

In a certain light, realizing his mistake was the real point of
this man's retreat. The desire to conquer impermanence by unit-
ing the self with an idealized and unchanging "other" is very understandable. It manifests in love as well as in religion and is a
persistent theme warned about in Buddhist psychology. Concentration meditations, deployed in the extreme, tend to take people
away, akin to what happens when one is lost in music or trans-
ported during sex. The mind becomes focused, physical sensations
are heightened, and feelings of serenity become strong. With dili-
gent one-pointed practice, these feelings of absorption can be extended for prolonged periods of time, giving people the impression
that all of their problems have disappeared forever. In his own

version of advice not given, the Buddha was careful not to urge his followers too far in this direction. Clinging takes many forms, and the desire for inner peace can sometimes be just as neurotic as other, more obvious addictions. The wish to lose oneself, however well intentioned, masks a mind-set dominated by self-judgment and self-deprecation. It is often just another way of trying to find a safe place to hide, replacing a troubled self with something perfect and unassailable. Right Concentration steers in a different direction. It offers stillness, not just as respite, but as a way of entertaining uncertainty. In a world where impermanence and change are basic facts of life, the willingness to be surprised gives one a big advantage.

I have tried to communicate this to my patients by not promising too much from meditation. Suffice it to say, I know there are reassuring experiences lying in wait for people and I know that concentration is one avenue for their awakening. How it will manifest for any given individual, however, is anyone's guess.

A good example of this comes from Dan Harris, a news anchor and journalist at ABC News, who has become a friend. Dan reached out to me after an unfortunate incident in which, while reading the news on *Good Morning America*, he suddenly and inexplicably dissolved into a puddle of nervous tics while mangling the words he was saying. One minute he was cogently presenting the news and the next minute he was blabbering incoherently as he grew more and more flustered. Dan came to understand that he had had a panic attack in front of millions of people on live TV, but in the moment he had no idea what the problem was. In his own way, he was exhibiting puzzling "conversion" symptoms like the ones

Dr. Nemiah had taught me about. Some kind of unprocessed anxiety was resurfacing in the form of perplexing physical symptoms,
embarrassing him on a national stage.

Months after the event, after seeking professional help and at
the urging of his wife, who had once read one of my books, he
came kicking and screaming to meditation. He called me out of
the blue, told me he was a reporter, and asked if we could meet up.
I agreed, we had a series of meals together over the next year
during which he asked good questions that made me think, and we
became friends. I had the sense, despite his hesitations, that he
would get a lot out of meditation and that it might be useful in
dealing with his anxiety. The panic attack made him realize that
he did not really know himself very well. I urged him, after a series
of conversations, to go on a retreat to see what might happen. I
thought it might give him another way of probing the unconscious.

Dan had an experience of Right Concentration on his first retreat. After five days of intermittent difficulty in which he often
questioned taking my advice, Dan took a chair from his small bedroom and sat out on the balcony at the end of his hallway. The retreat was in Northern California, and I imagine it was a beautiful
day. Sitting outside was a little easier for Dan, I think, than sitting
in the meditation hall. He was a bit more relaxed and not quite as
judgmental as he usually was: about the place, the practice, the
other people, and the vaguely New Age language that was being
thrown about by the instructors. For whatever reason, Dan's concentration kicked in while he sat on the porch. He did not see light
or feel love, as I had, but he felt as if something had clicked, as if he
had finally tuned in to the right frequency. He had the same kind
of effortless experience that I had had in my first retreat, in which

I was able to stay focused at will. "I'm not trying, it's just happening," he later wrote. "It's so easy it feels like I'm cheating. Everything's coming at me and I'm playing it all like jazz. And I don't even like jazz."

Dan spoke to me about all this when he returned. He was very moved by what happened next. Sitting there in concentration on the balcony, settling into his breath, he suddenly heard a loud rumble approaching. It began to increase in intensity, as he later put it, "like the fleet of choppers coming over the horizon in that scene from *Apocalypse Now*." His focus was strong, and Dan remained still as the rumble intensified. When he eventually opened his eyes, the roar crashing all about him, a hummingbird was hovering just in front of his face.

In Dan's book, this moment with the hummingbird is incidental. He had other powerful experiences on his retreat that he has described in *10% Happier*—experiences that fit more closely with traditional descriptions of what happens under the spell of concentration—but for me his encounter with the hummingbird, as a harbinger of what concentration was capable of delivering, is special. I do not think Dan's mind had ever been so still. This stillness enabled him to drop his guard and his filters, to open and relax in a way I'm not sure he ever had before. It gave him momentary freedom from his chronic coping posture: a defensive and wary tension, peppered by sarcasm, which had contributed to his panic attack on air. And the hummingbird was like a confirmation of his opening. It was as if the external world had recognized his attunement and touched him with a bit of its grace.

This is one of the great gifts of Right Concentration. We think we know things so well, but all it takes is a few days of watching

one's breath to show us what we don't know. I could never have
anticipated that a hummingbird would have been the vehicle for
Dan's breakthrough; he had to check himself into the retreat for
the mystery to unfold. But I knew that if he got himself there
something interesting would eventually happen and that he would
be taken by surprise. Right Concentration has given me that confidence.

In my time as a psychiatrist, I have seen the fruits of concentration take many forms, few of which I could ever anticipate. One
interesting example comes from a depressed patient of mine who
was drawn to meditation but did not feel able to do it alone. An
accomplished cellist, Eric's difficulty was not that he lacked discipline. When he had to learn scores for a performance, he was able
to apply himself like the professional he had become. He never
quite articulated what his problem was with meditation, but somehow I thought I understood. Eric did not feel safe with himself. He
was afraid of falling apart. He came to several public talks and
workshops and found that meditation was fine when he was part
of a group. Although he liked it and thought it could help him,
he would not do it alone. He tried a couple of times but never really gave it a chance. When his mind began to wander after the
first five minutes, he would give up.

I kept this information filed away and continued with Eric's
treatment. His depression improved and he began to see friends,
read, and work again. But there were still times when he was
turned inside out by his feelings, when for long stretches of time
he felt empty, cold, unmotivated, and uncomfortable. One day, we

had a session in which he told me he had no appetite, that the mere thought of cooking or buying food made him disgusted. The idea of handling a piece of chicken or a raw piece of fish turned his stomach. He had gone through his refrigerator and thrown out everything that was there: the onions, celery, and carrots he was saving for chicken soup. He wasn't hungry. Black coffee, cigarettes, and whiskey were enough for him.

I was concerned. I often talked to Eric about food, inquired what he was eating for dinner, asked where he was going to eat with his friends. He was divorced and lived alone and he worked a lot; if no one was preparing dinner for him, he was unlikely to think about what he might eat beforehand. Usually, if I talked about it enough, I could get him to lighten up a little. He had an artist's sensibility and most artists I know appreciate food, enjoy cooking, and are good at it. He was no exception. If I set the table, eventually he would join me for the meal. But on this day, I could not really get a spark going. At the height of his depression, he had compared it to dragging around a dead horse. That was the feeling of the session. The dead horse was back in town.

I asked Eric if he would like to meditate with me.

"Oh, yes," he responded.

Eric knew that I did not usually mix meditation with therapy and he thanked me for stretching myself. I asked Eric to be aware of the in breath at the tip of the nose and to say the word "in" when he breathed in, to notice the out breath when he exhaled and to say the word "out," and to feel the sensation of his two lips touching, repeating the phrase "touching, touching" after the out breath during the pause that is usually there before the next inhalation. Whenever his mind wandered, or rather whenever he noticed his mind wandering, I asked him to bring his attention back to the raw physical sensations of the breath. We did this together for about ten minutes, eyes closed, and when we stopped he had a bit of a smile on his face.

"I feel a little hungry," he said. "A few rumblings."

Of course, there was the possibility that Eric was just responding to suggestion. He knew I was concerned about his lack of appetite. Patients often want to please their therapists—there is a phrase for this in therapy: "flight into health." But I had the feeling his feeling was real.

The next day Eric did it at home. I think the clarity and simplicity of my instructions and the successful practice in my office made it seem possible. Eric understood that he could touch his depressed feelings lightly but take refuge in the breath. He described his experience to me in detail at our next session.

At first, Eric said, he began to weep. He sat down in his chair and began to weep. It did not stop and he did not understand what he was weeping about. It just poured out of him. Painfully. But he worked with the breath as best he could and maintained his resolve. Eventually the weeping subsided. In his mind's eye, Eric saw his sadness congeal into a dense black disc or ball. The ball had a faint aura of light around it, but its general feeling was bleak: a mixture of self-loathing and disgust, it had the flavor of the session the day before when the thought of eating made him sick, when he was dragging around the dead horse. As he moved his attention back to the breath, the black disc began to break up. It dispersed into many tiny pieces and seemed to disappear. He settled into the breath for a while with a sense of relief, but then, as he was coming out of the meditation, he saw the whole thing come back together again in a succession of magnetic jerks.

"Not so fast," Eric thought to himself, as he watched his pain reestablish itself.

But then he had a flash. He thought of two upcoming pieces he had agreed to play. Meaningful pieces, in which he was being asked to play new music with other dedicated and accomplished performers.

"How lucky I am to be able to do such a thing," he thought to himself, and he felt a temporary brightening of his mood.

When he relayed all this to me during the next session, he had a further inkling.

"The black disc," he said, "is desire. It's what I've done to it. Hopeless."

Eric was in his early fifties and was without an intimate relationship. Somewhere within, after his divorce, Eric had decided to eliminate desire. If he was not going to find someone to be with, there was no point in having it. This was protecting him from further disappointment but was also deadening him. We spoke of how his enthusiasm for his work contained the seeds of his desire, of how meditation had spontaneously shown that to be the case. This was important because it was a new thought. To feel desire still operating through his work—in a productive way, no less—was good. His desire was good. There was a trace here of something he needed. A neglected aspect of the self was now reestablished in his mind's eye.

For Eric, Right Concentration did not make his depression go away (for that we needed antidepressants); it helped him get un-

derneath it. Eric's emotional range was narrowed and compressed
by the aversion he had toward his feelings. First desire, and then
depression itself, had made him shut down. There was an element
of dissociation in Eric's depression, just as there was in Dan
Harris's panic attacks and in Dr. Nemiah's patients with conversion hysteria. The unbearable nature of his unfulfilled desire had
caused him to disconnect, creating new symptoms. When Eric
began to shift his focus to a neutral object, however, things opened
up. Concentration allowed him to see that the black disc of depression was not just depression. There was a light in it he had never
seen before. If I had suggested this to Eric beforehand, he might
well have rejected it out of hand. But when he came upon it himself, out of the simple task of watching his breath, it was as astonishing as the hummingbird had been to Dan Harris.

In my own experience, this tendency of Right Concentration to
foster a sense of connection is something I have always treasured.
I was reminded of this on a recent retreat where I was fortunate to
have an experienced teacher, a Swiss man who had once been a
monk in the Thai forest tradition. I met with him for ten minutes
after two or three days of meditation and confessed to him that I
was straining in my attempt to find the breath. It was subtle, but I
knew this tendency and could not always help myself. I was trying
a little too hard. Breath by breath, I was out in front of my experience, pulling at the in breath and forcing the out breath in an effort
to capture them fully. I was not practicing with Right Effort—some
kind of insecurity was making me strain and, in so doing, I was
missing the point.

The instructor listened patiently to my report and then gave
the simplest of replies.

"Don't chase her. Let *her* find you," he said with the faintest of smiles.

I was startled at the way he spoke. He had a bit of a German accent and I wondered if maybe I had heard him wrong, or if his English was not quite right. But at the same time I knew he was onto something. He gendered his comment that way on purpose. The concentrated feeling I was remembering and trying to refind was definitely a feminine one; it required a yielding, not a reaching. Whether this is simply because I am a man and the sensations evoked by one-pointed attention to the breath feel so "other" that I cannot help but eroticize them, I do not know. But there is a relationship between the spiritual and the erotic that Right Concentration helps to bring out. When the breath comes into focus, there is a settling that brings a retinue of relief. The traditional texts compare it to a healing jewel or to a medicinal balm, while secret esoteric works are more explicit about the erotic nature of what can happen. Neuroscientists talk about the brain's endogenous opiate receptors being flooded. Whatever the explanation, I knew this teacher understood me. And I could not help but see as I talked with him that my straining after the breath had its correlates in my erotic life as well.

I followed the Swiss teacher's advice for the next couple of days.

"Don't chase her; let her find you."

I went about my business with a little more aplomb thereafter. One afternoon, several days later, I was in the dining room in the late afternoon having tea. I was getting bored with the food (every day the same things were put out at five o'clock in lieu of an evening meal: rice crackers, tahini, peanut butter, raisins, sunflower seeds, and a big bowl of chilled fruit) and I began to wonder what would happen if I put the rice crackers in the toaster. Would they go *snap, crackle, pop?* I asked myself. One of the most common distractions on a retreat like this are old commercials or bits of songs that come floating out of the past like pulverized chunks of asteroids in the movie *Gravity*. Playing back old Rice Krispies jingles from my childhood gave me a rather pleasant feeling of nostalgia.

Amused by my musing, I suddenly felt something strange, something peculiar, something soft, cool and silky, sweet to the touch, hovering just out of reach. What was it? I had a moment of not knowing, like when the phone rings in the middle of a nap and you don't know where you are or what the sound is that is pulling you awake. Then I knew. It was the breath. It had found me. By itself. Just as the Swiss ex-monk had said it would. It was clear and soft and intensely pleasurable. I quickly released myself from my toaster fantasy and settled into the sweetness of the breath. It was no longer difficult to concentrate and I relaxed in my seat in the dining hall only a little surprised at the next feeling to come welling up inside. Gratitude. It was a feeling of gratitude.

There are different ways to interpret meditation breakthroughs, different ways of giving them import. For some people, the sense of peace may be what they are seeking, and that is enough. But for me, my experience in the dining hall carried another message. My usual modus operandi is an effortful one. My father once told me that, after my first books were published, someone wanted to know what I was like when I was young. I think they had a false image of me as some kind of prodigy of relaxed awareness.

"Well," said my father, trying to remember me as a child,

reaching for something concrete he could say, "he always did his homework."

This defined me as much as anything, and if I had to summarize myself I might give a similarly flavored response. I am identified with my striving and with the worries, responsibilities, and tensions that come with it. The retreat showed me that, however helpful this could be in the practice of meditation, to be overidentified with this aspect of myself obscured other, more mysterious, even erotic qualities I did not know were there. Getting out of my own way, letting *her* find me, opened me in a way I could not make happen through my own deliberateness. The paradox, of course, was that this non-doing was my own doing, too.

What is left when we are no longer identified with the personality we know? This is something the Zen tradition—indeed, all Buddhist traditions—is constantly seeking to convey. For me, on this retreat, the revelation was that I did not have to be the effortful person I thought I was. And when I wasn't this person, I did not disappear. Something filled me. I was filled by something. An unconscious potential became conscious.

There is a tradition in Japan of Zen teachers writing a poem at the moment of death revealing the essence of their understanding. One of my favorites is by Kozan Ichikyo, written in 1360 when he was seventy-seven years old.

> *Empty-handed I entered the world*
> *Barefoot I leave it.*
> *My coming, my going—*
> *Two simple happenings*
> *That got entangled.*

This empty-handed, barefoot feeling is what brushed up against me on the retreat. Right Concentration was the vehicle it rode in on. More than the relaxation it evoked, this feeling in the dining hall hinted at who I might be if I wasn't who I thought I was. With my homework out of the way, I was free to dwell in its mystery.

EPILOGUE

Suzuki Roshi, the founder of the San Francisco Zen Center and one of the first ambassadors of Buddhism to the United States, had a very helpful way of describing the relief that comes from getting over yourself. He used the expression "mind waves" to describe the turmoil of the ego's struggle with everyday life. Waves, he would always insist, are part of the ocean. If you are trying to find the peace of the ocean by eliminating the waves, you will never succeed. But if you learn to see the waves as part of the whole, to not be bothered by the ego's endless fluctuations, your sense of yourself as cut off, separate, less than, or unworthy will shift. This is a very particular way of dealing with the human sense of personal inadequacy, one that is strikingly different from the Western psychotherapeutic approach that seeks to uncover neurotic emotional patterns and excavate early childhood experience. In the Buddhist system, change comes by learning to shift one's perspective. Self-preoccupation, after enough practice, gives way to something more open. The ego's instinctive favoring of itself is eroded by a sense of the infinite.

Suzuki's point is that, know it or not, we are already equipped to meet whatever befalls us. Life's challenges are challenging, but there is room for faith, for confidence, even for optimism. The Western approach, seeking to strengthen the ego, focuses exclusively on the wave. Suzuki was always favoring the ocean. Buddhism often counsels meditation practice as the primary vehicle for awakening this shift in perspective, but at some point it becomes clear what is meant by the word "practice." Meditation is not an end in itself. It is not a quick fix. It is practice for life.

After forty-plus years, I can say for sure that I am not cured, nor am I enlightened. People continue to complain at times about my coldness, my aloofness, and my irritability. I still have to deal with the various kinds of suffering that plague me, with my own tensions and anxieties, with my own need to be right and my own need to be liked, issues that have been with me for as long as I can remember. And now, in my sixties, there are things to face I have never experienced previously. But I do have something I did not have before. It is not exactly inner peace. Nor am I really any happier than I ever was. Happiness, to me, seems to have a set point, like a thermostat, around which we hover, no matter what we do. But I now have the means, thanks to both Buddhism and psychotherapy, to face whatever life throws at me.

While in many ways I have remained the same—my personality is much as it ever was—I am not the prisoner of my ego that I once was. When the most difficult aspects of my character surface,

I know there is something I can do to not be at their mercy. While my three-year-old, seven-year-old, or twelve-year-old selves may not have given up the ghost, I do not have to be their helpless victim. Life has shown me where I have control over my own mind and where I do not. And I do not have to be cured to be hopeful. It is this optimism that I most want to make possible for my patients.

Buddhism is all about releasing oneself from the unnecessary constraints of the ego. Every aspect of the Eightfold Path is a counterweight to selfish preoccupation. But the Buddhist reprieve is accomplished not by leapfrogging over the ego's needs or demands, but by zeroing in on them: acknowledging and accepting them while learning to hold them with a lighter, more questioning, and more forgiving touch.

As I bring Buddhism more directly into my clinical work, this is the aspect I find most helpful. From my own experience, I know that even the most disturbing material loses its hold when successfully observed without attachment or aversion. The more I can be present with the entire range of my own and my patients' thoughts and feelings, the less we have to be run out of the room by them. In empowering the mind's ability to observe dispassionately, the Buddha found a hidden mental resource, one that a successful psychotherapy also taps. In working with this understanding, I know that in encouraging my patients to be real with themselves I can also help them to be free.

What I try to convey to my patients is that they can meet the challenges life throws at them by changing the way they relate to them. This is advice I now feel free to offer. The goal is to meet the challenges with equanimity, not to make them go away. When

Suzuki Roshi said not to be bothered by the waves' fluctuations, he meant it. And one thing we can say for sure. Life gives us endless opportunity to practice. Mostly we fail. Who can say they are not bothered by anything, really? But when we make the effort, the results can be astonishing. In an insecure world, we can become our own refuge. Our egos do not have to have the last word.

Acknowledgments

To Ann Godoff, for advice freely given, cheerful encouragement, support, clear ideas, and the willingness to steer me through the writing of this work. To my patients, who have trekked to my office week in and week out and trusted me with the intricacies of their inner lives. To those friends and patients who generously reviewed and approved the case material presented herein. To Robert Thurman and Sharon Salzberg, for inspiring me when we teach together. To Anne Edelstein, my literary agent, for bringing this book to the right publisher. To Sherrie Epstein, my mother, for allowing me to report on our always enlivening weekly conversations. To the founders, teachers, and staff of the Forest Refuge in Barre, Massachusetts, for creating a space for the silent retreats described in this book. To Dan Harris, for making me think, and Andrew Fierberg, for listening. To Casey Denis, for her extremely helpful notes. To Sonia and Will, for their humor, energy, enthusiasm, and love. To Sheila Mangyal, for taking care of all of us. And to Arlene, who makes everything possible and fills our lives with an ever-expanding sense of possibility. I love you.

Notes

Introduction

5 **"bears in his bodily frame the indelible stamp"**: Charles Darwin, *The Descent of Man* (1871), chapter 21.

6 **"Great Perfect Mirror Wisdom"**: For more on this, see Yamada Mumon Roshi, *Lectures on the Ten Oxherding Pictures*, trans. Victor Sōgen Hori (Honolulu: University of Hawaii Press, 2004), p. 5.

7 **Mara remained a force**: Stephen Batchelor, *Living with the Devil* (New York: Riverhead, 2004), pp. 16–28.

7 **After the ecstasy**: Jack Kornfield, *After the Ecstasy, the Laundry* (New York: Bantam, 2001).

8 **An aged Chinese monk**: Jack Kornfield, *A Path with Heart* (New York: Bantam, 1993), p. 154.

17 **Path is there to be cultivated**: Stephen Batchelor, *After Buddhism* (New Haven, CT: Yale University Press, 2015), p. 83.

Chapter One: Right View

31 **"Don't make such a big deal"**: All unattributed quotations from Arlene Shechet are from her correspondence with Jenelle Porter, December 22, 2014, in preparation for Jenelle Porter's *Arlene Shechet: All at Once* (Munich/London/New York: Delmonico Books–Prestel and The Institute of Contemporary Art/Boston, 2015), pp. 12–31.

35 **Some translators use "realistic"**: See Robert A. F. Thurman, *Essential Tibetan Buddhism* (New York: HarperCollins, 1995).

35 **"not a recipe for a pious Buddhist existence"**: Batchelor, *After Buddhism*, p. 127.

Chapter Two: Right Motivation

42 **Engler, has a story**: Engler's story about Munindra was relayed to me in personal correspondence. It was reproduced in my *Open to Desire* (New York: Gotham, 2005).

43 "dharma means living the life fully": For more on Munindra, see Mirka Knaster's *Living the Life Fully: Stories and Teachings of Munindra* (Boulder, CO: Shambhala, 2010).

46 "Oral rage": I presented a truncated version of this episode in *Thoughts without a Thinker* (New York: Basic, 1995), pp. 170–72.

53 Winnicott wrote of how inevitable failures: See, for instance, Donald W. Winnicott, *Babies and Their Mothers* (Reading, MA: Addison-Wesley, 1988).

55 a famous paper of Winnicott's: Donald W. Winnicott, "Hate in the Counter-Transference," *International Journal of Psychoanalysis* 30 (1949), pp. 69–74.

56 "However much he loves his patients": Ibid., p. 69.

56 "A mother has to be able": Ibid., p. 73.

Chapter Three: Right Speech

69 "Each of us tells ourselves": Sharon Salzberg, *Faith: Trusting Your Own Deepest Experience* (New York: Riverhead, 2002), p. 1.

70 "an ambient, opaque silence": Ibid., p. 3.

70 "The story I was telling myself": Ibid., p. 3.

71 "You know what your problem is": Ibid., p. 5.

71 "Just showing up": Ibid., p. 16.

71 "participate, engage," and "link up": Ibid., p. 16.

72 "For when all is said and done": Sigmund Freud, "The Dynamics of Transference" (1912), in *Standard Edition of the Complete Psychological Works of Sigmund Freud*, vol. 12 (London: Hogarth, 1958), p. 108.

72 "You can do anything you want to do": Amy Schmidt, *Knee Deep in Grace: The Extraordinary Life and Teaching of Dipa Ma* (Lake Junaluska, NC: Present Perfect, 2003), p. 58.

78 "Amid the howling wind": Mason Currey, *Daily Rituals: How Artists Work* (New York: Knopf, 2013), pp. 90–91.

79 talking with my eighty-eight-year-old mother: This discussion was first published in my article "The Trauma of Being Alive," *New York Times*, August 3, 2013.

Chapter Four: Right Action

87 "Acceptance of not knowing": Donald W. Winnicott, "Mind and Its Relation to the Psyche-Soma" (1949), in *Through Paediatrics to Psycho-Analysis* (London: Hogarth, 1975), p. 137.

88 "Learn the backward step": Heinrich Dumoulin, *Zen Buddhism: A History; Volume 2: Japan* (New York: Macmillan, 1990), p. 79.

93 Huike says to Bodhidharma: Andre Ferguson, *Zen's Chinese Heritage: The Masters and Their Teachings* (Somerville, MA: Wisdom, 2011), p. 20.

94 The mind's empty, aware nature: Joseph Goldstein, *Mindfulness: A Practical Guide to Awakening* (Boulder, CO: Sounds True, 2013), p. 314.

97 "Flirtation, . . . as a social art form": Michael Vincent Miller, *Teaching a Paranoid to Flirt: The Poetics of Gestalt Therapy* (Gouldsboro, ME: Gestalt Journal Press, 2011), p. 116.

98 "My analyst looked up briefly": Louise Glück, *Faithful and Virtuous Night* (New York: Farrar, Straus and Giroux, 2014), p. 38.

Chapter Five: Right Livelihood

106 four kinds of happiness: Nyanaponika Thera and Hellmuth Hecker, *Great Disciples of the Buddha: Their Lives, Their Works, Their Legacy* (Boston: Wisdom, 2003), p. 352.

109 "Right Livelihood is not only about": Goldstein, *Mindfulness*, p. 387.

114 a murderer named Angulimala: For more on this story, see my *Going to Pieces Without Falling Apart* (New York: Broadway, 1998), p. 56.

Chapter Six: Right Effort

123 "Tell me, Sona": Nyanaponika Thera, *Aṅguttara Nikāya: Discourses of the Buddha* (Kandy, Sri Lanka: Buddhist Publication Society, 1975), p. 155.

125 "The rule for the doctor": Sigmund Freud, "Recommendations to Physicians Practicing Psychoanalysis" (1912), in *Standard Edition of the Complete Psychological Works of Sigmund Freud*, vol. 12 (London: Hogarth, 1958), p. 112.

126 "It must not be forgotten": Ibid., p. 112.

128 "To put it in a formula": Ibid., p. 115.

137 "The basis of the treatment": Donald W. Winnicott, "Two Notes on the Use of Silence" (1963), in *Psycho-analytic Explorations* (Cambridge, MA: Harvard University Press, 1989), p. 81.

139 "a child, an invalid, one in the flush of youth": Richard Gombrich, *Theravada Buddhism* (New York: Routledge, 1988), p. 64.

Chapter Seven: Right Mindfulness

151 "With excessive thinking and pondering": "*Dvedhāvitakka Sutta*" (chapter 19), *The Middle Length Discourses of the Buddha: A Translation of the Majjhima Nikāya*, trans. Bhikkhu Ñānamoli and Bhikkhu Bodhi (Boston: Wisdom, 1995), p. 208.

Chapter Eight: Right Concentration

177 good example of this comes from Dan Harris: See Dan Harris, *10% Happier* (New York: HarperCollins, 2014).

179 "I'm not trying, it's just happening": Ibid., p. 138.

179 "like the fleet of choppers": Ibid., p. 138.

187 "Empty-handed I entered the world": Yoel Hoffman, *Japanese Death Poems* (Boston: Tuttle, 1986), p. 108.

Epilogue

189 describing the essence of the Buddhist approach: Shunryū Suzuki (Suzuki Roshi), *Zen Mind, Beginner's Mind* (Boston: Shambhala, 1970, 2006).

Index

The Trauma of Everyday Life

Trauma does not just happen to a few unlucky people; it is the bedrock of our psychology. Death and illness touch us all, but even the everyday sufferings of loneliness and fear are traumatic. In *The Trauma of Everyday Life* renowned psychiatrist Mark Epstein uncovers the transformational potential of trauma, revealing how it can be used for the mind's own development.

"In a breathtaking display of the therapeutic art, Epstein does ingenious psychodynamic detective work.... *The Trauma of Everyday Life* reads like a gripping mystery, one told by your warm and reassuring, but utterly candid, analyst." –Daniel Goleman, author of *Emotional Intelligence*